CW00496041

Workplace Learning:

Have we got it all wrong?

Alexander Fahie

Copyright © 2023 Alexander Fahie

All rights reserved.

ISBN: 9798865032625

DEDICATION

For Zoe

Workplace Learning: Have we got it all wrong?

Contents

Acknowledgements

This book would not be here without the support, interest and input of so many people. From those who unknowingly inspired me to the score of experts that volunteered their time. My understanding of the subject has been shaped by reading the following authors – many of whom I am fortunate to have spoken with while writing this book. These include but are not limited to Charles Handy *"The Second Curve, Thoughts on Reinventing Society"*, Nigel Paine, Josh Bersin, Adrian Wooldridge *"The Aristocracy of Talent" and* Dan Pink *"Drive: The Surprising Truth About What Motivates Us"*. James Lovelock, *'Novacene',* Dr. Jac Fitz-Enz's *"The New HR Analytics: the Economic Value of Your Company's Human Capital Investments" and* Donald Clarks', *'Artificial Intelligence for Learning: How to use AI to Support Employee Development'*.

I am acutely indebted to the following experts helped me better understand and frame the central tenet to this book; Andrew Stotter-Brooks (*Vice President, Learning and Development Etihad Aviation Group*), Roberta Sawatzky MA, CPHY, GPHR (*Professor, Okanagan School of Business),* Dr Ashwin Metha MBA, MChem (*Global Learning Technology Leader, Bayer Corp*), Patrick Dunne (*Chair: Boardelta, EY Foundation, ESSA*), Pamela Dow (*COO, Civic Future*), Guy Stephens (*Head of Microlearning, IBM*), Andrew Collier (*Global Learning Director, Campari Group*), Jonathan Eighteen (*Global Head, Consulting and Advisory Services, NIIT*), Steve Margison (*Global Leadership Development and Head of Coaching, Philip Morris International),* Donald Clark, (*CEO and Wildfire Learning*). Dr Buruk Koyuncu (*SVP, Leadership Development, LHH*) and Nick Shakleton-Jones (*CEO and Founder, Shakleton Consulting*). Please note that the places of work were accurate at time of writing.

I am also grateful to the team, academic board, directors, shareholders, and users of Ethical Angel and Interactive Tutor for their faith and patience to allow me to collect and document my thoughts in this way. Startups are busy places, so being afforded the time like this is a real luxury. One team member in particular, Henry Butters, was invaluable in helping me to get the project started.

Many thanks to my beta readers Bernadette McDonald, Chris Ridley, Ditte Fahie, Guy Stephens, Gemma Glover, Matthew Addisson Black, Efraim Lerner, Caroline Woodrfuff, Alexandra Kodjabachi, Philip Murdoch and Roberta Sawatzky.

Finally, to my family, friends and fiancée, Zoe - your constant support, belief in my work, and encouragement were instrumental in seeing this project through. This book wouldn't have been possible without your backing. Thanks for everything.

Foreword

I have had the distinct privilege of witnessing the author's remarkable expertise, unwavering passion, and dedicated commitment in crafting the narrative of this transformative message.

As a Human Resource specialist, I find immense joy in sharing insights and knowledge with aspiring minds eager to navigate the intricate tapestry of the business world. My journey, from years spent in various industries, including not-for-profit, private business, and government, to my current role as a tenured Business Professor, has allowed me to observe the evolution of training and development methodologies—from the traditional 'sage on the stage' to the more contemporary 'guide on the side.' While there is still much ground to cover before learning and development become a truly individualistic, human-centric endeavour, we are undeniably making strides in that direction.

Since 2009, as a learning and development coach, my interactions with individuals seeking personal and professional growth have been centred on a strengths-based approach. Hearing their stories, understanding their dreams, and navigating their challenges offer a profound glimpse into their identity and potential. Designing individualized development plans tailored to their unique strengths is a privilege, representing an opportunity for business leaders to cultivate the next generation of powerful and passionate individuals who will collectively propel us forward in this dynamic era of work.

To the reader embarking on this enlightening journey, rest assured that you are in the capable hands of an expert whose dedication to the art and science of learning is truly unparalleled. The wisdom encapsulated within these pages is not only informative but also transformative, providing a nuanced look into the author's rich tapestry of experience and knowledge.

May this book serve as a source of inspiration, a catalyst for personal growth, and an empowering guide to embracing the transformative power of continuous learning and development. As you delve into the chapters ahead, may you discover not just knowledge but a steadfast companion on your unique journey of growth and discovery.

With appreciation and admiration,

Roberta Sawatzky MA, GPHR

Introduction

"Learn continually – there's always "one more thing" to learn!"
– Steve Jobs

My name is Alex, and I am obsessive. I feel I should come clean with you from the outset, both to explain and excuse what is to come. For me, this book is not just an exploration; it's more of a therapeutic release, a cathartic exorcism of a passion I've had for a while now. The challenge of workplace learning.

This obsession started in 2019, when I read the results of a study conducted by Docebo, a learning management software company. The results revealed what I felt was a startling fact, **"87% of millennials in the workforce feel that their learning experience is boring and not relevant?"**[i].

At first glance, one may be tempted to dismiss this incendiary statistic as mere click-bait, designed to grab attention and lure in potential customers. After all *sensationalism* is the order of the day. However, it resonated with me on a profound level. It ignited a concern, a nagging doubt that made me ponder: Could workplace learning genuinely be facing such a crisis?

And crisis is the right word. After all workplace learning isn't merely about skill acquisition. It's about safety protocols for engineers, instilling ethical cultures, and more. It's the cornerstone of personal and corporate growth. From the factory floor to the boardroom, learning and development "L&D" is the umbrella term for all activities designed to improve the capabilities, characters and performance of employees. When a significant chunk of the workforce finds L&D experiences uninspiring, it's more than a red flag; it's a call to for us all to reevaluate and revamp.

If only, because a failure in workplace learning affects its people and the bottom line. At the heart of every successful company lies an efficient, skilled, and motivated workforce. When L&D initiatives are implemented effectively, they not only boost an individual's skills but also elevate the collective competence of the organisation. This translates directly into enhanced operational efficiency, innovative solutions, and a competitive edge in the market, all of which are critical drivers of profitability.

"When you invest in upskilling and reskilling, you reduce the risk of turnover, attract higher quality talent, and empower your best employees with the tools and resources they need to stay sharp. According to LHH, more than half of organisations report increased levels of both employee productivity and loyalty after participating in training/upskilling programs"[ii]

However, if L&D initiatives come across as tedious, irrelevant, or misaligned with employees' professional aspirations and the company's goals, there's a risk of a disengaged workforce. Disengagement can lead to increased turnover, lower productivity, and missed business opportunities - a costly proposition for any organisation. What is more, if workplace learning practitioners are forced into short-term objectives, to fit in with quarterly reporting and budget appraisals we run the risk of judging outcomes on vanity targets, as Donald Clark says, "If you are worried about bums on seats you are looking at the wrong end of the learner".

The problem with vanity metrics is that they obfuscate the real impact of workplace learning behind pigeonholed goals like attendance and completion rates. Can bums on seats ever really equate to a return on learning investment, is this yet another alarm bell that leaders, shareholders, and L&D professionals cannot afford to ignore?

The pursuit of knowledge and understanding is one of the most fundamental aspects of human nature. From the earliest stages of childhood, we are constantly asking questions, seeking to make sense of the world around us, and striving to learn and grow. Yet, despite this innate drive, the field of learning in the workplace continues to be shrouded in confusion as to its purpose, ownership, value and application.

I began to ask questions like, why do we have learning and development programs in the first place? What is their real purpose? And are we doing it right? It soon became clear to me that there was much more to this field than I had ever imagined or personally experienced.

This book is a reflection of my journey so far, written without jargon and as objectively as my passion allows. Each chapter is an essay that explores a different aspect of workplace learning, drawing on research, expert interviews, and my own experiences and observations. Together, these essays seek to answer a simple question, "**Workplace Learning: Have we got it all wrong?**".

In the following chapters, we will define the purpose of workplace learning, demystifying it from the shroud of pseudoscience that's enveloped it. Then we will explore a history of workplace learning, considering influences from around the world.

From there, we will then investigate the now, seeking to understand the current objectives and challenges of employers, employees and the learning practitioners themselves. The book culminates by envisioning a future state, with possible solutions, maybe even some actionable insight, that you could take back into your workplace.

By sharing my obsession with you, challenging the effectiveness of workforce learning, I hope to ignite discussion in corporate corridors. To bring to the forefront the undeniable role of workplace learning — not merely as an instrument for personal and intellectual development, but also as a linchpin in an organisation's trajectory for success.

i. Demystifying Workplace Learning

"The more that you read, the more things you will know, the more that you learn, the more places you'll go." - Dr Seuss

Education and Learning

In order to effectively explore the efficacy of workplace learning, we first need to centralise and clarify the myriad of definitions and terminologies that cloud its understanding. A confluence of mystifying descriptions, that to the uninitiated act as a masonic capture impeding our ability to comprehend and critically assess it. So, for our first step, lets work out what workplace learning actually is.

The pediment of workplace learning is supported by the twin pillars of ensuring employee *education* and creating opportunities for *learning*. Though frequently used interchangeably 'learning' and 'education' are distinct concepts and should be considered accordingly. Think of them less as being two sides of the same coin but separate currencies entirely. As Nick Shakleton-Jones says, "Education is something that is done to you. Learning is something you choose to do." Education has an imposed structure, a start and an end, think of it as a carefully mapped expedition with a clear route and all the reference points and distances marked. Whereas learning is more of an individual's personal odyssey into the unknown. To seek new experiences and to interact with new environments. Engendering them with skills and behaviours that'll determine how they navigate life.

Education in the workplace is instrumental in ensuring that employees possess the necessary knowledge to perform their duties effectively and compliantly. Like our school experiences, this type of training reflects the disciplined rhythm of our childhood. A conveyor belt of processed information ingestion and regurgitation. Education adheres to a scripted syllabus with prescribed goals, usually delivered through instructor-led training sessions, online courses punctuated by quizzes, or obligatory reading. Picture factory workers being trained on machinery operation, industry captains gathering at conferences to informed of the latest trends, or employees securing certifications and qualifications pertinent to their roles. Although workplace education is necessarily targeted, there is inherent value of the educational process itself. Roman Philosopher, Seneca the Younger remarked, "Study, not to know something else, but to know better".

Almost two millennia later, in 1921, Albert Einstein echoed this sentiment. When Thomas Edison declared a college education to be of no use, Einstein retorted, "The gathering of facts is not the primary function of a college. One could learn them from books. The true merit of a liberal arts education lies not in the absorption of numerous facts, but in the conditioning of the mind to think independently, something that textbooks alone cannot provide"[iii]. Seneca and Einstein both hint at the essential role of education in triggering the learning process.

Within a workplace setting, it isn't enough for employees to simply recall and regurgitate specific information gained through education. They need to cultivate a wider range of understanding that can only be acquired via the curiosity of learning rather than through direct instruction.

Learning is an inherently active process, fuelled by the individual's direct engagement. If we imagine a rock concert, learning isn't the audience member, listening on the side-lines, instead, it is the performer, engaging wholeheartedly in the act. It is energetic, constant even creative.

> *"Learning is not a spectator sport. Students do not learn much just sitting in classes listening to teachers, memorizing pre-packaged assignments, and spitting out answers. They must talk about what they are learning, write reflectively about it, relate to past experiences, and apply it to their daily lives. They must make what they learn part of themselves."* - Chickering, Arthur W. and Ehrmann Stephen C[iv]

Learning is the consequence of our surroundings. How we are exposed to and exchange with it. These interactions and experiences develop our knowledge, skills, behaviours, characters and qualities. Although Chickering and Ehrmann's reference is rooted in higher education, their notion seamlessly extends to the sphere of the workplace. The role of workplaces, therefore, is to ensure that their employees aren't mere onlookers; but encouraged to take centre stage, actively participating with their surroundings, to benefit and learn from their experiences and interactions. As the ancient Chinese proverb goes, "Tell me, I'll forget - Show me, I'll remember - Involve me, I'll understand".

If we briefly delve into the science of learning, we find that fundamentally it is about transforming information into memory, ready for recall when the situation demands. Interestingly, there's a deep-seated connection between learning and emotion – events that stir our feelings tend to leave a more enduring imprint on our memory than their more neutral peers. Hardly surprising when we consider the trials and tribulations of our earliest ancestors and their daily quests for survival. Remembering what plants make you sick, which animals are likely to bite and how to keep warm were essential life lessons. I like this explanation by neuroscientist Mary Helen Immordino-Yang, "Emotion is not just something that happens to us or that we express; it's something that helps us learn"[v]. The reason for this is that emotions stimulate the amygdala, a region of the brain responsible for forming memories. This explains why certain smells, feelings, or experiences can trigger recollections. For me, the smell of cinnamon will always conjure up memories of my Swedish grandmother, 'Mormor' and her home on the hill just outside Stockholm. If we take this belief through to the specific focus of this book it implies that for workplace learning to be truly effective, it ought to stir emotional responses.

Both employee education and learning are critical for the workplace, each offering unique benefits. Education imparts job-specific competency through a structured curriculum, while learning fosters a range of professional and personal skills through exposure and exploration. However, there is a fundamental challenge to imparting education or stimulating learning. The workforce is made up of individuals and no two individuals are alike. A range of personal idiosyncrasies and experiences will determine how people interact with their surroundings, what they find stimulating and emotive. There are even those who go further and argue that each of us has an inclination for a particular learning style. Perhaps, the way we learn is preordained or is it just another case of neuro myths and pseudo-science? Let's find out.

Neuro Myths and Pseudo Science

D espite ancient knowledge of the brain's central role in intelligence, it is really in the past 20 years that modern neuroscience has truly flourished. Yielding significant insights into how the brain functions. "Fuelling many of these discoveries was the Human Genome Project, which sequenced and mapped our genes in 2001, and the NIH Blueprint for Neuroscience Research, a group of 14 NIH Institutes and Centres that support and advance the area of neuroscience"[vi], which was created in 2004.

The reach of neuroscience's accomplishment has also extended to our learning strategies. Through a better understanding of neural mechanisms, workplace learning practitioners and educators have been able to design learning interventions that align with the brain's natural functioning. For instance, recognising the role of spaced repetition in training, as "repetitions—if well designed—are very effective in supporting learning."[vii] Or, creating programs with repeated exposure to information over intervals, otherwise known as the spacing effect. "The spacing effect is one of the oldest and best documented phenomena in the history of learning and memory research."[viii]. Additionally, insights into the role of emotions and the brain's inclination for problem-solving, have all emerged from recent neuroscientific research.

Yet, along with the invaluable knowledge gleaned from authentic research, a host of misunderstandings and unfounded theories have become, whether through ignorance or pervasive forces, common *knowledge*. These "neuro myths" are at best, inclined to simplify the intricate processes of the brain excessively or at worst... utter rhubarb.

A prominent example, is the myth of learning styles. You've probably heard of learning styles; you may even have taken a test to determine which type of learner you are. It's a wonderful idea – elucidating why certain people flourish in certain scenarios. Yet, despite considerable evidence contradicting the existence of learning styles, "In fact, the considerable evidence that exists directly contradicts this theory"[ix], this theory continues to shape the framework of instruction in education and workplace learning environments alike.

It was in the 1950s, that the term *learning styles* entered the education lexicon through the academic literature of Herbert Thelen. In the 1970's the term was built on by David Kolb, who designed the learning style inventory (LSI), introducing four learner types: 'accommodator', 'converger', 'diverger', and 'assimilator'.

But it wasn't until the 1980's that the learning styles myth really began to take root in our workplaces. Neil Fleming, an educator from New Zealand, formulated the VARK model during his tenure as a school inspector. The model, which stands for Visual, Aural, Read/write, and Kinaesthetic, categorises distinct learning preferences and has greatly influenced pedagogical approaches. Interestingly, Fleming himself was influenced by the US educator Walter Burke Barbe, who introduced VAK in the 1970s. But it was really Fleming's contribution that popularised the learning styles myth.

Fleming later recounted, "I noticed that, in response to a question such as *How do I get to..?*, people gave directions in different ways. I wondered if different people prefer to be told how to get there in different ways - being shown a printed map, having a map sketched for them, being told, being given written instructions, being physically taken there. So, I began with a question about this"[x].

Advocates of learning styles propose that by catering to the distinctive preferences of the learner or student, we can create an ecosystem where learning doesn't merely occur - it flourishes. Those who actively promote the idea of learning styles, are let's be frank, often consultants or companies commoditising the concept. They classify learners into categories such as visual, auditory, and kinaesthetic, among others, arguing that these groups reflect unique cognitive processing modes. They explain that some individuals lean towards a hands-on approach, others prefer to learn through auditory or visual means. Depending on which purveyor of goods and services you explore, the count of distinct learning styles range from 4 to 12. I guess the more there are the more courses can be sold. But for the sake of expedience, let's explore the most popular seven discrete learning styles and how you might want to interact with them:

- **Visual Learners:** They find visuals the most effective medium for learning. Trying to instruct them about data analysis? Infographics can work wonders.

- **Auditory Learners:** They're inclined towards auditory learning. To explain the key features of a new marketing campaign, a podcast could be your best bet.

- **Logical Learners:** These problem solvers love crunching data. To help them learn, provide exercises that apply the newly acquired knowledge.

- **Verbal Learners:** Written or spoken words are their ideal learning tools. To elucidate new company policies, a manual or a lecture could be apt.

- **Kinaesthetic Learners:** They believe in experiential learning. A factory tour could be a practical way for them to understand a new product.

- **Interpersonal Learners:** Group dynamics facilitate their learning. A group activity for a new team-building exercise could be beneficial.

- **Intrapersonal Learners:** They thrive on solitary learning. An online course that they can progress through at their own pace might suit them best.

Whilst sceptics, like me, brandish their pitchforks and social media commentary of disapproval, dismissing the concept of learning styles as a myth, contending that our brains are far more versatile, capable of assimilating information in myriad ways, this labelling is inherently attractive. "The tendency", Scott Barry Kaufman, an American cognitive scientist explains, "to classify and categorise objects is a deeply ingrained aspect of human nature"[xi]. We like to believe there is a codified reason for who we are, to know what we are and, what that means. But, when we put people into strict bandings, we often overlook the variety within each group and exaggerate the differences between them. A human flaw not consigned to workplace learning. Everyone is unique, with their own traits and life experiences. So, we should be careful about letting labels distort our understanding of each other and using them to diagnose and deliver learning.

Dr. Tesia Marshik, in her awesome TED talk, *Learning styles & the importance of critical self-reflection*, draws attention to the deep-seated belief in learning styles - a belief she argues still held by a substantial majority, "including 93 percent of British teachers" [xii]. She presents a compelling argument, backed by extensive research, that challenges the existence of learning styles. As Michael Zwaagstra, a senior fellow at the Fraser Institute says, "This [learning style] experiment has been carried out multiple times and the results are always the same—there's no statistically significant difference between the people who learned something according to their so-called learning style versus those who did not. The individual learning styles theory is little more than an urban legend—again, a myth" [xiii]. Critics argue that the evidence base for different learning styles is tenuous at best, and may inadvertently pigeonhole learners, creating self-limiting beliefs. Remember Einstein's fish? "Everybody is a genius, but if you judge a fish by its ability to climb a tree, it will live its whole life believing that it is stupid".

According to Marshik, this belief's pervasiveness is partially attributable to its inherent attractiveness. Learning styles theory presents an appealing narrative, celebrating individual differences and suggesting that we can enhance education by tailoring it to each student's unique learning style.

Marshik argues that just because an idea feels good or sounds appealing, it doesn't necessarily mean it's accurate. Despite its popularity, there's a significant lack of empirical evidence supporting the learning styles theory. Most scientific studies don't substantiate the claim that tailoring instruction to individual learning styles results in better learning outcomes. Instead, they reveal that different teaching methods prove effective for different types of content, regardless of the learners' preferred style. I do feel some sympathy for Fleming, who as the architect of VARK has become the *de facto* figurehead of the Learning Style theory. Fleming once said, "Learning styles have had a bad press. It seems that they are lauded and then attacked on an almost cyclical basis. This is probably because it is very difficult to measure learning (in part because it is difficult to define learning in useful ways), especially if one wants to know when learning happens or to what it can be ascribed"[xiv]. Well, we can't do anything for bruised egos, but how do these myths take root?

A few years ago – *unrelated to workplace learning* – I visited the doctor, convinced I had all the symptoms of some exotic ailment I had only discovered from scrolling YouTube. So convinced was I, and so strong the evidence of its existence, that I was ready to write my own prescription (I had avidly researched treatment) and all the Doctor was needed for was rubber stamping. With the internet and access to hundreds of articles, videos, blogs and papers, who even needs doctors I congratulated myself – already imagining a new product of self-diagnosis for general release.

The reason why is VOMIT and confirmation bias. VOMIT stands for, Victim of Modern Information Technology, and when paired with confirmation bias –the tendency to interpret new evidence as confirmation of one's existing beliefs or theories[xv] is a toxic cocktail self-perpetuating a cycle of ignorance. Kahneman explains it, "contrary to the rules of philosophers of science, who advise testing hypotheses by trying to refute them, people seek data that are likely to be compatible with the beliefs they currently hold"[xvi]. An example of this can be seen as recently as 2004, when Frank Coffield led a thorough investigation into Learning Theory literature, "his team identified an astonishing 71 different models or ways of classifying learning styles, and they compiled a wide array of associated journal articles, magazine features, websites and conference papers, few of which were peer-reviewed or conducted in well-designed studies"[xvii].

As it transpired, my diagnosis was wrong, I was just suffering from a common cold. The analogy here – and why I expose myself before you - is that just as in self-diagnosis, individuals believing in the learning styles myth often unconsciously seek and prioritise supportive evidence while turning a blind eye to the contrary. As Marshik says, "another reason that this belief exists is confirmation bias, that natural tendency we have as humans that we want to be right"[xviii]. In other words, we see what we want to see.

From my perspective, the truth may well be nestled somewhere in this tug-of-war's middle ground. We all employ different 'learning styles' under different circumstances and at different times. Imagine your workplace as a vibrant, dense jungle brimming with daily challenges and opportunities that require skilful navigation. In such a terrain, the Darwinian principle of survival of the fittest comes into play ensuring the need for adaption – to use all the different approaches to learn what we need to thrive and to avert failure. After all, we humans are highly adaptable creatures, and our capacity for learning in various ways is arguably one of our greatest strengths.

Another pervasive neuro myth pertains to the concept of 'brain hemisphere dominance.' This notion suggests that individuals are either left-brained (analytical and logical) or right-brained (creative and intuitive). As Dr Sarah McKay says, "This popular notion was debunked in 2013 by University of Utah neuroscientists who used brain imaging to show there is NO evidence that people are 'right-brained' or 'left-brained'"[xix]. Instead, our brains are significantly more interconnected, with most tasks demanding cooperation between both hemispheres. "It's absolutely true", says the Neuroscientist Dr Jeff Anderson, lead author of the study, "that some brain functions occur in one or the other side of the brain. Language tends to be on the left, attention more on the right. But people don't tend to have a stronger left- or right-sided brain network"[xx].

A significant driver of these neuro myths is pseudo-science - theories that might look and sound scientific but lack the rigorous testing and validation at the heart of genuine scientific research. These pseudo-scientific claims often draw from isolated studies or anecdotal evidence or oversimplify complex research findings. In a workplace learning context, these claims can lead to training programmes that promise instant solutions or groundbreaking results. The reality, however, often falls far short of these lofty promises. Perhaps you've experienced this yourself?

The perpetuation of these myths and pseudo-scientific principles is, in no small part, due to commercial interests. Companies, consultancies and influencers exploit these misunderstandings to sell products, programmes, and services that supposedly enhance learning based on neuro myths. The thing is, they actually might believe that what they are promoting is real. "It is undermining the credibility of our industry when we have all of these different theories that have been debunked", says Dr Kuva Jacobs, "yet heads of learning are continuing to spread these myths on LinkedIn, they get a lot of visibility… people who don't know any better see it on social media and that myth continues to propagate." We have to do our research and challenge these myths. Just because a company, vendor or influencer is extolling its virtues and authenticity – it doesn't mean that it is. Afterall, for a very long time we believed that the earth was flat, that smoking was a cure for congested lungs and that carrots help you see in the dark. In promoting such myths, these parties are adding to their implied legitimacy. Fuelling widespread acceptance and integration of pseudo-scientific principles in workplace learning vernacular. As Marshik argues, "this not only wastes valuable resources but also risks harming employees' learning outcomes and development".

As practitioners, commentators, or even just as lifelong learners, it is our responsibility to challenge new concepts and theories before we put them into practice. The complexities of the brain and the dynamics of learning deserve nothing less than an approach grounded in legitimate, robust scientific research. For now, we can dispel these neuro myths and pseudo-scientific theories that might seek to divert our investigation into the effectiveness of workplace learning. In the future, at the very least, ubiquitous debunking and cold-shouldering of these myths will result in fewer brain-training apps claiming to boost general intelligence, or professional development workshops that supposedly customise training to individual learning styles or brain hemispheres. A positive outcome for everyone.

Knowledge, Skills and Behaviours

As we've already explored, there is much "confusion surrounding the terms 'education', 'development' and 'learning,' to the point where they are often used interchangeably"[xxi] . But adding to this perplexity, is the frequent use of knowledge, skills and behaviours (qualities) as synonyms of learning goals. To fully appreciate their unique value and how they all fit in, we must distinguish between these concepts. Pamela Dow, COO of Civic Future and former Executive Director at the UK Cabinet Office responsible for the Civil Service curriculum, explains.

> *"Knowledge is what everyone has to learn and internalise to be effective. Skills are the core administrative skills we need, like communications and data analysis, specialist-level stuff that has to be learned for us to be useful in our roles. But qualities and behaviours are ethical things, things you can say that you have in an interview that aren't easy to disprove."*

Knowledge is often regarded as a primary measure of workplace competence. Resulting in a binary evaluation - one either knows how to do their job, or they don't. The fallibility of judgement aside, we can argue that knowledge in a workplace setting encompasses accumulated facts, guiding principles, and insights sourced from both their formal education and hands-on experience. This repository of information not only educates individuals about their specific sectors but also offers a theoretical framework that propels action.

Skills represent the application of this knowledge. They are the practical tools and techniques used to execute tasks and navigate professional challenges. But, when you think about the skill sets that drive success, what comes to mind? Is it the expertise of a coder, the precision of an engineer, or the insights of a data analyst? These are undoubtedly vital. But there's another set of skills - often dubbed 'soft' - which have for too long been overshadowed by their 'hard' counterparts.

Would you believe me if I were to tell you that soft skills were invented by the U.S. Army? That empathy, adaptability and communication were instruments of the greatest military on earth. Well, you shouldn't. Soft skills were of course not a martial mechanism, but, way back in the 1950s, the U.S. Army did seek a way to efficiently categorise and train skills.

In 1959, the U.S. Army channelled significant resources into tech-driven training methodologies, aiming to enhance operational workflow and learning efficacy. They crafted a set of guiding principles dubbed Systems Engineering of Training (CON Reg 350-100-1), which established a blueprint for developing specialised courses tailored to unique Army roles. Enter behavioural scientists like Paul G. Whitmore, who said that "the courses created under this regulation would cover job related skills"[xxii].

Perhaps jaded by Hollywood, but my imaginings of the U.S. Army does not lend itself to envision a group of burly war veterans discussing soft skills as we understand them today. And in truth, they weren't. As we can see from below excerpt, the definition of soft skills has evolved considerably:

"The CONARC regulation on systems engineering (CON Reg 350-100-1) of training defines "soft skills" as: job related skills involving actions affecting primarily people and paper, e.g., inspecting troops, supervising office personnel, conducting studies, preparing maintenance reports, preparing efficiency reports, designing bridge structures."[xxiii]

At the 1972, CONARC Soft Skills Training Conference, Whitmore and other behavioural scientists joined with US Armed Forces personnel to discuss soft skills. Whitmore and his colleague John P. Fry presented three papers dealing with skills analysis and training procedures, defining, evaluating and positioning soft skills. But during the conference, military leaders were also called upon to share their experiences. One such presentation caught my attention, and that was made by Lieutenant Colonel Mike Lyman, the commanding officer of the Infantry School systems engineering group at Fort Benning. Colonel Lyman had been directed to undertake the "Eight Combat MOS Study"; an experiment aimed to systemise training across four major combat arms. The goal? To identify common tasks *fundamentals* that transcended specific Military Occupational Specialties (MOS's) and ensure more streamlined, efficient training.

To tackle these challenges, Lyman proposed a pretty revolutionary approach where tasks were compartmentalised, thereby making the employment of soft skills more measurable. He also sought to define the desired outcomes and consequences of task performance, emphasising the importance of understanding the broader impact of soft skills on unit missions. In the presentation's conclusion Colonel Lyman said, "I hope I have in this short period given you an idea of how we're systems engineering soft skills in the Eight Combat MOS Study I feel it is an exciting study and it will have a tremendous effect on all training conducted in units"[xxiv].

As the value of soft skills was recognised, they naturally evolved to suit the needs of different environments. There is Afterall little call for 'designing bridge structures' in a grocers or factory. With this evolution came new language, "power skills", "vocational skills" or as Seth Godin postulates, "real skills"[xxv]. However, you prefer to call them, I believe the best definition of them goes back to Whitmore, who said, "In other words, those job junctions about which we know a good deal are hard skills and those about which we know very little are soft skills."[xxvi]

Beyond knowledge and skills, we have behaviour and qualities. What Aristotle refers to as moral character. Aristotle argues that, to act virtuously, is not merely to perform a right action but to be in a righteous state of character. "Anyone can get angry – that is easy – or give or spend money; but to do this to the right person, to the right extent, at the right time, with the right aim, and in the right way, that is not for everyone, nor is it easy."[xxvii]

Overlaying this philosophical viewpoint on the corporate world it suggests that the *essence* of an employee's value is not solely in their accomplishments but also in the integrity and character they bring to the table. "People who exercise judgment," notes Barry Schwartz, a visiting professor at University of California, Berkeley, Haas School of Business, "do much better work and are much more satisfied."[xxviii] Embodying the right behaviours at work, therefore, isn't about ticking off a list of acceptable actions, but about cultivating a consistent moral disposition.

"There's an overemphasis on competencies and compliance and then under an underinvestment in qualities" says Patrick Dunne, who holds several non-executive director roles, including chair of the EY foundation, "and if you look historically at the organisations that did super, super well over a sustained period, they invested a lot in character." Just as Aristotle highlighted that virtues like courage, honesty, and wisdom were central to leading a fulfilled life, businesses today recognise that these very virtues, when embedded in workplace behaviour, can drive both individual growth and employer success.

Character acts as the bedrock of an employees' professional identity. It's where core values, ethical beliefs, and personal integrity reside, guiding choices and shaping one's professional compass. And, it's a virtue recognised by employers. Whilst "good character fits no familiar psychological pattern" [xxix], if you were to ask hiring managers, *good character,* in line with the employer's values is the ultimate indicator of a good fit. As Dunne recalls, "so, we've recruited people who weren't necessarily a perfect fit for the job, on the basis of skills, but they've got the character we can give them the skills." This is a sentiment shared by Elon Musk, controversial founder and CEO who recounted at the South by Southwest Conference, "[My biggest mistake is] weighing too much on someone's talent and not someone's personality...it matters whether someone has a good heart."

Whilst Aristotle recognises the challenges of developing one's character, "science suggests that our character and behaviour can be drastically altered by new circumstances or passions" [xxx]. John Rawls, the American philosopher, introduced the idea of 'reflected equilibrium' as a tool for character development. Rawls' argues that a deliberative process of introspection and reflection we can align our character more closely with our desired moral and ethical ideals. This is an idea we will come back to later in the book.

As Dow positioned at the start of this chapter, competencies, namely knowledge and skills, represent objective, largely measurable prerequisites for job efficacy. In contrast, elements like behaviours, character, and innate qualities - what I like to refer to in a workplace setting as *'tradecraft'*- are more subjective, nuanced, and challenging to quantify. Yet, they're pivotal in honing employees to excel in their roles. Consider two salespeople: both possess equivalent product knowledge, but one excels in relationship-building, empathy, and strategic conversation steering. This individual, having honed superior tradecraft, achieves more sales. The same example can be adjusted to just about any role, or position in the workplace.

Language

The ambiguity of language is a common theme throughout this chapter. Despite the evidential credence given to workplace learning by its prevalence and positioning on business websites and job advertisements, its true purpose remains ambiguous. We know it's important, but do we all know what it is for? This confusion is not limited to us; professional bodies and experts within the workplace learning arena have offered various definitions, further complicating matters.

For instance, the Association for Talent Development (ATD) describes learning and development as, "a field of practice that focuses on the acquisition of knowledge, skills, and competencies required to perform effectively in the workplace"[xxxi]. Similarly, the Chartered Institute of Personnel and Development (CIPD) defines it as "the activities that help individuals develop their skills, knowledge, and abilities, and provide the resources and support necessary to perform their roles effectively"[xxxii].

Both the Association for Talent Development and the Chartered Institute of Personnel and Development emphasise the importance of equipping individuals with the knowledge, skills, and competencies necessary for effective workplace performance. ATD narrows its

28

description of learning and development to being a *field of practice*, focusing strictly on the "acquisition" aspect. In contrast, the CIPD offers a broader perspective, highlighting not only the development of skills, knowledge, and abilities but also underscoring the provision of "resources and support" that enable individuals to excel in their roles.

The variety in definitions may stem from evolving ownership and influence within the realm of learning and development. Over time workplace learning has transformed to keep pace with changes in the workplace and society at large. In recent history, it primarily represented task-oriented training for specific roles and functions, as well as education and testing to ensure compliance with regulatory requirements. In this earlier stage, learning and development functioned as a tool of human resources, aligning employee development with HR policies and practices such as performance management and compliance.

However, as the world grew more connected and organisations became more intricate, the need for a specialised field dedicated to fostering learning became evident. This led to the emergence of the Learning and Development (L&D) department, marking a significant evolution in organisational structures. The L&D department had a key role to play: to facilitate continuous learning and upskilling within the workforce, keeping pace with the rapidly evolving business landscape. From conducting routine training sessions to devising strategic talent development plans, L&D became the driving force behind a company's learning culture.

As the L&D department took root, it served as a bridge between the employees and the management, aligning individual learning goals with the company's strategic objectives. It sought to harness the collective intelligence of the organisation, foster collaboration, and promote knowledge sharing. Despite the crucial role of the L&D department, it has faced significant challenges in keeping pace with an increasingly complex and rapidly evolving world. As the wealth of knowledge grows exponentially, sifting through and selecting the most relevant information for the workforce becomes a herculean task. Simultaneously, the shift towards remote work, flexible working hours, and the increasing diversity in the workforce has brought new challenges in delivering effective learning experiences. Nigel Paine recognises this and asserts that, "Learning and development must be focused on the challenges of today, not the challenges of yesterday"[xxxiii]. This idea is echoed by industry analyst Josh Bersin, "The whole field of corporate training and development is ripe for reinvention... We need to rethink our approach to learning; build a new mindset and change the way we think about training", we will hear more from Josh later.

One significant factor contributing to the ambiguity surrounding workplace learning is its need to constantly adapt to shifting demands. This adaptation spawns a duo of issues. Firstly, as we've already explored, the growth of pseudoscience, which, in an attempt to legitimise the ever-evolving realm of workplace learning, introduces a plethora of jargons and terminologies. Often accompanied by a wave of new products, use cases and consultants advocating for the latest models. An attractive proposition, as Dr Emrah Düzel, of UCL Institute of Cognitive Neuroscience says, "When we see something new, we see it has a potential for rewarding us in some way. This potential that lies in new things motivates us to explore our environment for rewards. The brain learns that the stimulus, once familiar, has no reward associated with it and so it loses its potential. For this reason, only completely new objects activate the midbrain area and increase our levels of dopamine."[xxxiv] In other words, newness quite literally feels good.

The second issue arises within businesses themselves; as new departments are formed with distinct reporting lines, fresh leadership often seeks to establish its identity and protect its budget by distinguishing themselves from predecessors. Often embracing new approaches, goals and concepts. The end result? A cacophony of unfamiliar terminologies enters the workplace learning lexicon, further obfuscating its purpose for the uninitiated.

An analogy I like, that demonstrates confusion stemming from linguistic divergence can be traced right back to the biblical story of the Tower of Babel from the Book of Genesis. In this narrative, all of humanity shared a common language, which became a source of their collective strength. Their ambition and potential, came from a unifying clarity, they understood each other perfectly and were consequently able to do the unthinkable. To construct a tower, so perfect, so high that it would challenge divine supremacy itself. As the story unfolds...

> [5] *God came down to look over the city and the tower those people had built.*
> [6-9] *God took one look and said, "One people, one language; why, this is only a first step. No telling what they'll come up with next—they'll stop at nothing! Come, we'll go down and garble their speech so they won't understand each other." Then God scattered them from there all over the world. And they had to quit building the city. That's how it came to be called Babel, because there God turned their language into "babble." From there God scattered them all over the world.* — *Genesis 11:1–9*[xxxv]

This parable offers a salient parallel to our modern situation. In the world of workplace learning, as new terminologies and pseudo-scientific theories emerge, we risk creating our own 'Tower of Babel' scenario. Our shared understanding, the foundation of our collective progress, could become obfuscated. If unchecked, this can hinder the very progress we aim to achieve, just as in the Tower of Babel story.

The more I explore the intricacies of workplace learning, the more I'm convinced it's not just an isolated discipline but a pivotal component seamlessly intertwining with overarching organisational goals. This sentiment mirrors Leadership Development consultant David DeFilippo's thoughts, "The role of L&D is to partner with the business, to grasp its strategy, and then shape capabilities to realise that vision." DeFilippo isn't just talking about concocting programs; he's alluding to a harmonious relationship between workplace learning and the wider business landscape.

Yet, several roadblocks hinder this harmonisation. Financial constraints often handcuff ambitions, while the absence of workplace learning leaders from top-tier decision-making tables can curtail their potential influence. Additionally, I've observed a somewhat insular behaviour among workplace learning leaders; in that their frequent interactions are mostly limited to counterparts. "L&D had a tendency to disconnect itself from the business life and ebb and flow of the organisation in order to produce stuff, courses, content or whatever" Says Dr Nigel Paine "Companies who tell you that if you are in L&D and if you focus on their product, their solutions, that's the job done... that feeds into the we're self-contained, we produce these great services and therefore you begin to huddle inwardly". This self-imposed echo chamber can cloud perspective, promote learning myths and potentially leading to strategies misaligned with broader business challenges. But, Dr Paine warns, "evaluating their own content and has no real reference to the outside world".

In an effort to sidestep the potential befuddlement arising from diverse interpretations in workplace learning, we will use the following definition shared by Steve Margison when I interviewed him:

> *"The purpose of learning and development is to help execute business strategy".* - Steve Margison

With these concepts, myths and language demystified, we are ready to begin our exploration. Like a Dickensian novel we will explore the past, present and future of workplace learning. First stop, the ghost of workplace learning's past. By delving into the history of workplace learning, we will appreciate the influences from different times and places. Recognising how workplace learning evolved and better arming us to challenge whether workplace learning is employing the right approaches today to equip employees with the necessary tools to effectively execute business strategy.

Part 1. The History of Workplace learning

"For most of human history, the skills you needed to learn were the skills you needed to survive. So, it was a much more hands-on, experiential type of learning. The big change came when we moved from an agrarian economy to a more industrialized one. Then, you needed to learn very specific skills to thrive in that environment. And so, you had the rise of formal education, the rise of vocational training, the rise of the modern school system, and that has persisted to this day." Dan Pink

Carl Sagan, the astronomer is perhaps best known for being the designer of the first physical messages for space. Inscribed on a golden record aboard the two Voyager spacecraft launched in 1977, the disks are designed to communicate with any potential extraterrestrial life:

> *"a present from a small, distant world, a token of our sounds, our science, our images, our music, our thoughts and our feelings"* – President Jimmy Carter.

They are a time capsule of human history – an audio-visual collection intended to portray the diversity of life and culture on Earth. When envisioning how to reflect the myriad of human achievement, Carl said, "you have to know the past to understand the present". So, inspired by NASA's approach to cosmic promotion, we too will start our exploration of workplace learning at its very beginnings, returning to the source from where it all originated.

My hope, is that by looking at how workplace learning evolved over time and around the world, we should get a sense of how it evolved and from where aspects of it as we know it today were influenced. But where to start? Frankly, there are dozens or peoples, states and epochs from the rich tapestry of human history from where we could have started our journey to reveal the practices of workplace learning. Many of which affect the programmes of today. But, in the spirit of brevity and focus, I've whittled it down to a select few.

I invite you therefore to join me on a grand tour through the Medieval period, following in the footsteps of Marco Polo across the commercial arteries of Europe, the intellectual capitals of Islam, the fantastically exotic provinces of China, right to the extraordinarily unique islands of Japan.

From there, we'll make leaps forward in time in our Tardis of workplace exploration to the smokestack-lined, smog filled horizons of the Industrial age, we'll witness the advent of Globalisation in the aftermath of the Second World War and lastly, we'll revisit the tumultuous sea of the recent past, digesting the unprecedented storm of the COVID era.

Our first stop is the Medieval period, a time often dismissed as a cultural lacuna between the grandeur of the antiquity and the intellectual efflorescence of the Renaissance. Some will be incredulous that I didn't start my historical probe into workplace learning with the Father of Teaching, Socrates, or the orchestra of ingenuity demonstrated by various ancient states and peoples. For those who feel wronged, please accept my humble apologies. But, by way of explanation I believe I can make an argument that it was during this time, the Medieval period, that the first seeds of workplace learning as we know it today were, if not sown, cultivated *en masse*.

Around the world the Medieval period was a time of great change. Commerce, then as it does today, provided meritocratic reward for those who excelled at their craft and opportunities for risk takers. Traditional social hierarchies were supplemented with a new class of merchants and craftsmen. A class with money and ever-increasing influence. Trade, buoyed by new technologies and insatiable demand for more exotic goods, became global. Cities such as Timbuktu and Zimbabwe in Africa traded with their European counterparts, the nations of Islam and the Far East. Yet the trade was not just goods, but also ideas.

In Europe, the first university was founded in Bologna in 1088. The approach to schooling embraced by these forerunners of structured higher education was scholasticism. A method of learning that's known for rigorous conceptual analysis and the careful drawing of distinctions. Students engaged in disputations, a systematic and thoughtfully curated form of debate, with the purpose of uncovering and consolidate truths in theology and sciences.

A different approach emerged from the scholarly epicentre of Islam. Where Madrasa schools in North Africa and the Middle East teemed with illuminated manuscripts and ideas were actively exchanged, discussed and challenged. Here, scholars pioneered an innovative strategy, amalgamating blended learning and critical thinking.

In the vast terrain of China, we observe the genesis of stringent examinations, a principle that remains integral to our professional certifications today. Japan offered a distinctive angle to apprenticeship (yes, a nod to Karate Kid is inevitable) and fostered a culture of lifelong learning.

As we journey forward through time, we will examine the factors that influenced the development of workplace learning and how it has adapted to the ever-changing needs of society and industry. From traditional task-oriented training amidst the din of industrial age machinery, to the more holistic approach championed amid globalisation. As borders blurred, we were forced to learn new languages, both literal and figurative. Before finally exploring the effects of the coronavirus and the adaption of workplace learning.

This historical account has been a joy to research and will, I hope, offer insights into the evolution of workplace learning and how it continues to influence the sector today.

The Medieval Apprentice

E nvision, if you will, an era where the crux of workplace learning wasn't reliant on paper credentials or online courses, but rather steeped in hands-on experience, nurturing mentorship, and the unhurried, yet steady mastery of skills. This was the heart and soul of the medieval apprenticeship system. A system that not only served as the bedrock for a myriad of trades and crafts worldwide but also heralded the dawn of structured learning within the workplace.

So, one might wonder, how did this apprentice system take root? Picture the high medieval period, roughly stretching from the 11th to 13th century. During this time the population of Europe exploded, growing "from about 38.5 million people to about 73.5 million" xxxvi . Simultaneously, advancements in agricultural practices, such as crop rotation, and the advent of the humble wheelbarrow (mind you, this was not a European innovation but rather a gift from China with the earliest record of the wheelbarrow dating back 800 years prior). These developments spurred productivity. Subsistence farming became commercial agriculture as farmers were able to generate surplus crops and livestock more reliably. What they now required was a *marketplace*, as close to their ever growing consumer base as possible. Market squares and hills sprung up and around these bustling focal points, towns grew. Granted, this is a rather simplified explanation. A multitude of socio-economic factors played their part in the urbanisation of Europeans. But, what relevance this has to our exploration of workplace learning? Well, with the emergence of metropolises came wealth. And with wealth, came opportunities for an up-and-coming class of craftsman and artisans.

Technological marvels like the compass, cartography, and the astrolabe were revolutionising maritime trade and exploration. Unlocking new markets across the Americas, Asia, and Africa. As trade flourished and intercontinental exchanges became more frequent, there was an increased appetite for specialised goods. This surge in demand led to an explosion of creativity and craftsmanship, with artisans producing a wide array of products tailored to the idiosyncratic tastes and needs of those with money to spend. The resultant effect was the emergence of craftsmen as a dominant force in this new world order. Their skills and expertise became highly sought after, creating a thriving artisan economy. Their influence permeated every layer of society, from the royal courts of Europe to the bustling cities of Asia.

For better or worse it is human nature to protect what we have that is valuable. We put up fences around our land, castles at the borders of our kingdoms, and lock our most precious chattels away in vaults and safes. Even today, in technology entrepreneurship, we use 'moats' to protect our intellectual property from competitors. The burgeoning class of craftsman recognised that what they had was valuable. Their skilled hands wove the threads of progress and prosperity into the fabric of society, creating masterpieces that both met the needs of the day and echoed the spirit of the times. But it took time to become a master craftsman. Whilst a European could expect to complete their apprenticeship in seven years, spare a thought for those in Japan, where, "you're not considered a master of your craft *'Takumi'* until you've spent 60,000 hours refining your skills"[xxxvii], that's equivalent to working full-time for over 30 years. So, the last thing you'd want is for some upstart to undercut both the quality of your work and your prices.

To protect their positions and exert influence on behalf of their common interests, craftsman formed guilds. These were not just associations of tradespeople, but complex, self-regulating bodies that provided a framework for the development of apprentices. They had significant power, "guilds often had a great deal of influence over local governments. Guild leaders, especially those of powerful merchant guilds, frequently also served as local government officials"[xxxviii]. Guilds were not a new concept; the earliest examples can be found from antiquity in India and what we now call Iran. They can also be recognised in classical roman times as *collegium* (which were organised groups of merchants who specialised in a particular craft). But, it was in the medieval period that guilds flourished.

Perhaps their influence was most visible in the creation of the Hanseatic League. The Hanseatic League was a confederation of guilds from the low countries, across northern Europe to modern-day Estonia. Whilst not a centrally controlled state in the way we would understand it today it was a collection of separate merchant towns engaged in a highly constructed defensive and trade alliance. More akin to the European Union than a kingdom or empire, also, Britain chose not to join it then either. In a broader sense, guilds were instrumental in shaping the social fabric of medieval towns.

These guilds were more than just associations of skilled artisans; they were custodians of quality, guardians of the sanctity of their craft, protecting their revenue source and mitigating their reputational risk in the way a multi-national company does today. Ensuring quality, supply and nurturing budding talent through the apprenticeship system. Each guild set stringent standards for the goods its members produced, and rigorous training programs ensured that these standards, "low quality products were not tolerated because all guild members would suffer"[xxxix].

In 1563 the English Parliament passed the 'Statute of Artificers', which prescribed a system for working conditions, pay, and the relationship between the craftsman and the apprentice. The Statute "included conditions which could be likened to apprenticeship minimum standards today; Masters should have no more than three apprentices and apprenticeships should last seven years" [xl] . Contracts were obligatory, "binding servant to master and vice versa; in which the master personally taught the apprentice; took responsibility for the latter's moral welfare; and gave him board and lodgings"[xli]. An apprentice would learn not just the techniques of his trade, but the values of diligence, integrity, and respect for the materials and tools of their craft. This dedication to excellence reflected in the superior quality of goods produced by guild associates, further enhancing their reputation and protection from non-guild members.

We can identify the early foundations of mentorship, on-the-job training, and collaborative learning in these workplaces. The guilds were more than just associations; they were "essentially multifaceted social networks, valuable in building community and a sense of belonging"[xlii]. They were hubs where craftsmen passed down their trade skills, refining them with each generation of apprentices. This mirrors the way in which early humans, even before the establishment of formal schools, thrived on communal learning. Whereby essential skills like hunting, farming, or crafting were honed within collaborative groups where individuals observed, learned and practiced from and with one another. Fast forward to today, and we find contemporary organisations embodying these very principles, prioritising skill development through practicing internships, mentorship, and onboarding programmes.

In the words of author and thought leader Malcolm Gladwell, "Practice isn't the thing you do once you're good. It's the thing you do that makes you good"[xliii]. The medieval European apprenticeship system embodied this idea long before Gladwell articulated it.

> "Medieval apprenticeships were the original learning-by-doing experience. They offered young people a practical education, combining classroom learning with on-the-job training, and provided a pathway to social mobility and economic independence." – Bryan Caplan, Professor of Economics at George Mason University.[xliv]

Then as today, those teaching grapple with issues of motivation and engagement of those being taught. Challenges also faced but differently approached in medieval apprenticeships. In those times, apprentices were motivated by a blend of personal and professional growth, economic stability, and social standing, all guided by a master craftsman – and because they had to by indenture. Whilst the hierarchical structure of the trade and clear roadmap instilled ambition, with the end goal, the dangled carrot, being financial and social elevation as a master craftsman. There was also a weighty stick. Should an apprentice fail to complete their apprentice "he would not legally be able to work in his trade for another master". These medieval systems, though more rigid and long-term than today's flexible, multidisciplinary workplace learning programs, underscore the enduring importance of hands-on experience, mentorship, and instilling motivation to learn. Understanding the evolution of these systems can offer insights into crafting effective, modern-day learning and development programs.

Another notable difference lies in the accessibility and inclusivity of learning opportunities. Medieval apprenticeships in Europe were often limited to those from certain social backgrounds, "As long as your parents have a certain level of wealth, you can still become an apprentice (an income of at least 20 shillings a year from land or rents – roughly equivalent to 50 days' wages for a skilled craftsman in the early fifteenth century)" [xlv]. Faith and sex were also prerequisite conditions for membership, "guilds imposed a plethora of entry barriers against groups such as women and Jews" [xlvi]. In contrast, contemporary workplace learning initiatives strive to be more inclusive, offering opportunities for continuous growth to employees regardless of age, gender, or background.

Around the world medieval apprenticeship system provided a solid foundation for the acquisition of specific knowledge through hands-on experience and expert education. However, the learning that occurred within these apprenticeships extended far beyond the confines of the trade itself. Apprentices often gained invaluable, holistic skills such as customer interaction, recognising bad deals, developing relationships through networking, and going on to train others. In essence, they acquired tradecraft – the art of being great at what they did, not just knowledgeable about it. "Learning is an experience that has been honed for millennia," says Nick Shackleton Jones, author of *How People Learn: Designing Education and Training That Works to Improve Performance*, "At a simple level, we see learning taking place through guided practice, observation, and storytelling." These three activities were at the heart of the master-apprentice relationship for centuries. The observation came first, as the master had the apprentice simply watch for a considerable length of time. Observation was more vital than actual hands-on practice as materials and tools were in short supply and replacing either was at a considerable cost. Guided practice followed, with the master quick to find fault but also to praise as the apprentice started with the basics and slowly mastered the craft. Storytelling was the true tie that binds for the relationship between master and apprentice. It wasn't just the transference of knowledge or the mastery of skills, but the understanding of the craft on a personal level. The emotions that were tied to it. The way to treat a customer. The way to keep putting your heart and soul into it until you get it right. The little nuances that you would never understand if you hadn't walked the walk.

Let's look at the stories of two workers, John and Thomas, both of whom entered the same trade but experienced different opportunities for learning. John was fortunate enough to secure an apprenticeship, where he honed his trade skills and developed his tradecraft. Thomas, on the other hand, did not have access to such an opportunity, thus missing out on the crucial development of tradecraft.

Through his apprenticeship, John was immersed in the day-to-day operations of his master's workshop. He not only learned the technical aspects of his trade but also the soft skills needed to excel in his profession. John's master emphasised the importance of good customer service and taught him how to interact with clients in a professional and courteous manner. John soon understood that building strong relationships with customers was essential for maintaining a successful business.

Moreover, John's apprenticeship exposed him to the art of negotiation and recognising bad deals. He observed his master's interactions with suppliers and customers, learning to distinguish between fair and unfavourable transactions. This ability to recognise and navigate the intricacies of business dealings would prove invaluable to John as he progressed in his career and established his own workshop.

Networking and relationship-building were also central to John's development of tradecraft. His master introduced him to other professionals in their trade, and John began to forge connections that would benefit him in the future. He learned not just the value of collaboration, sharing knowledge, and expanding his professional network but also how to engage in conversation with his peers.

Finally, John's apprenticeship taught him how to train others. As he grew more proficient in his trade, he took on the responsibility of teaching younger apprentices, refining his ability to communicate complex ideas and provide constructive feedback. In essence, through exposure to his master John was learning the mindset of becoming a master himself.

In contrast, Thomas, who lacked the opportunity for an apprenticeship, struggled to develop his tradecraft. He gained knowledge of his trade through self-learning and informal mentoring but missed out on the comprehensive learning experience that an apprenticeship provides. Thomas faced challenges when it came to customer interaction, negotiation, networking, and training others, as these skills were not easily learned outside of the structured environment of an apprenticeship.

The stories of John and Thomas hig"ligh' the Immense value of apprenticeships in teaching not just the knowledge of a trade but also the tradecraft that contributes to overall success in a profession. Apprenticeships offered a holistic approach to learning, equipping individuals with the skills needed to excel both in their trade and in the broader world of work. As we reflect on the enduring relevance of the learning and development approach of medieval apprenticeships, we must recognise the importance of cultivating tradecraft alongside technical expertise to create well-rounded, adaptable, and successful professionals.

It was not just the trade of goods and raw materials that was opened up during this period but also the exchange of ideas. The 'Silk

Road', a term first coined by German explorer Ferdinand von Richthofen (uncle to the famous WW1 flying ace, 'The Red Baron') in 1877, describes a loose network of routes used by traders since antiquity. If like Venetian merchant, Marco Polo, we journeyed along this route from Europe in the Medieval period we'd have witnessed extraordinary sights and ideas that would influence our thoughts on a variety of things, including workplace learning.

Islam's Golden Age

O ccuppying the southern and eastern shores of the Mediterranean we'd have encountered the Islamic world, a rich society where the pursuit of knowledge was revered at the highest level. The madrasa, which literally translates as "a place where learning and studying take place"[xlvii], was used to denote both secular and religious educational institutions. Madaris were the fulcrum of intellectual life in the medieval Islamic world. Nestled within the bustling cityscapes, these institutions were more than just schools; they were vibrant hubs of knowledge and wisdom, where the torch of enlightenment was passed from one generation to the next.

Marco Polo, travelled through many countries, but his accounts – certainly in the earlier editions – are particularly bigoted and sensationalist about Islam. "It's not how "Muslims saw themselves", but how "Christian Minorities and Europeans saw Muslims": a look of mostly fear, misunderstanding, and hate", says Muhammad Arrabi, Principle Program Manager at Microsoft Research. However, a contemporary of Marco Polo's, the Moroccan scholar and explorer Ibn Battuta, paints a valuable impression of the medieval Islamic leaning landscape.

"The madaris of Cairo cannot be counted for multitude. As for the Maristan [hospital], which lies "between the two castles" near the mausoleum of Sultan Qala'un, no description is adequate to its

beauties. It contains an innumerable quantity of appliances and medicaments, and its daily revenue is put as high as a thousand dinars. "[xlviii] – Ibn Battuta

This account from Ibn Battuta captures the widespread institutionalism of the madrasa system at a time when the Islamic world was experiencing a 'Golden Age' of intellectual and cultural prosperity. From Timbuktu to Baghdad, the Madrasa, or Madaris (plural) served as incubators for a wide range of disciplines and it is interesting to note that scholars considered mathematics, philosophy, and law not as isolated branches of knowledge but as being intricately intertwined.

Madaris employed a holistic approach to learning that would not look out of place in the workplace of today. Scholars blended classroom-based training with discussion and hands-on experience. It was not merely an exercise in rote memorisation, or an unquestioning acceptance of established truths as enshrined in the Medieval apprenticeship system we've just explored. Instead, it encouraged critical thinking, fostering a spirit of inquiry and intellectual exploration.

This tradition of critical thinking was not born of this time; rather, its roots are deeply embedded in the foundations of Islam, evidenced by the Holy Quran itself. The scripture encourages believers to ponder, interpret, and apply its teachings to their day-to-day lives. A poignant example can be found in the narrative between a tyrant Pharaoh and a Muslim man, as depicted in *Sura* [40]*, Verse* [28]. It is written that despite the overwhelming power of the Pharaoh, the Muslim man provoked a thoughtful inquiry, underlining the essence of belief in Allah, as opposed to accepting Pharaoh as a god. He didn't initiate an assault on the Pharaoh, nor did he rise to defend Prophet Moses. Instead, he opted to stimulate a thoughtful discussion.

Similarly, Abraham encouraged his tribe to critically assess their practice of worshipping stone sculptures. "In forcing his tribe to examine their faith critically, they were able to identify their erroneous ways and recognise their transgressions against themselves", *Sura [21], Verses [66] and [67]*, without resorting to violence. In essence, critical thinking calls for the suspension of predetermined evaluations and emotions such as anger. What we would recognise today as emotional quotient "EQ", or in other words the ability to manage one's own emotions in a positive way "to relieve stress, communicate effectively, empathise with others, overcome challenges and defuse conflict" [xlix].

Abu 'Ali al-Husayn ibn Sina, better known in Europe by his latinised name *Avicenna,* is considered to be one of the most significant polymaths of this period. A Persian, born in 980 CE, he was "arguably the most influential philosopher of the pre-modern era"[l]. His encyclopaedias of philosophy would create a lasting influence on the Islamic world and, once translated, would have far reaching impact on scholasticism. His books cover natural sciences, logic, mathematics, metaphysics, theology and education.

In one of his books, Avicenna wrote a chapter, "The Role of the Teacher in the Training and Upbringing of Children"[li], for the benefit of teachers working at *Maktab* schools, what we'd recognise today as prep schools. In his writings, he postulated that an educational setting featuring collective instruction, as opposed to the personalised guidance provided by private tutors, holds the potential to bolster a child's learning efficacy. He gave several reasons for this, including the positive impact of competition and emulation among students, as well as the benefits of group discussions and debates. This learning approach that encourages critical thinking was picked up on by Carl Boyer in his book, A *History of Mathematics*:

"The Arabs in general loved a good clear argument from premise to conclusion, as well as systematic organisation – respects in which neither Diophantus (Ancient Greek mathematician, author of Arithmetica often heralded as the Father of Algebra) nor the Hindus excelled. The Hindus were strong in association and analogy, in intuition and an aesthetic and imaginative flair, whereas the Arabs were more practical-minded and down-to-earth in their approach to mathematics"[lii]. – Carl Boyer

In the realm of mathematics, Islamic scholars built upon the established works of Greek and Indian mathematicians, advancing them to new frontiers during the 9th and 10th centuries. The most famous of Madrasa based mathematicians from this period was al-Khwarizmi. In comparing him to Diophantus Boyer says, "the title [The Father of Algebra] more appropriately belongs to al-Khwarizmi". Al-Khwarizmi was best known for developing methods to solve linear and quadratic equations. We can appreciate the impact of his, 'calculating completion and reduction' by reading a translation of his own words for the breadth of its application; "inheritance, legacies, partitions, lawsuits, and trade, and in their dealings with one another, or where measuring of lands, the digging of canals, geometrical computation and other objects of various sorts and kinds are concerned"[liii]. His seminal book, *Kitab al-Jabr* or *Al-jabr wa'l muqabalah*, gave us the "new branch of mathematics bearing this name"[liv], algebra.

How much of an effect the madrasa system had on likes of al-Khwarizmi, and Avicenna is up for debate. What can be recognised is the value of the blended learning and critical thinking approach espoused by the Madrasa system. "Traditions of learning within the *dar-al Islam* (Islamic sphere of influence) privileged the spoken word over the written, reflecting the belief that information and arguments were best derived from words spoken by the actual author or, if that was not possible, from a teacher whose *isnad* (chain of transmission from the original author) was reliable"[lv]. A study by the Brandon Hall Group found that blended learning typically results in a 29% higher knowledge retention rate compared to traditional learning methods. Whilst the U.S. Department of Labor regards critical thinking as the backbone of crucial workplace abilities[lvi].

Even today, the influence of the Madrasa system permeates modern workplace learning. Just as the Madrasa system recognised the value of blending theory and practice, modern learning and development programs have embraced this approach to create well-rounded, skilled employees. The concept of continuous learning, a cornerstone of contemporary professional development, and critical thinking, echoes the Madrasa tradition of lifelong intellectual exploration. This emphasis on rational, sceptical, and unbiased analysis resonates with the spirit of inquiry fostered in Madaris, encouraging learners not just to accept, but to question, explore, and critique.

Now, we go further east.

Imperial China

L ying on his deathbed, Marco Polo, it is said, whispered a startling confession, "*I did not tell half of what I saw, for I knew I would not be believed*". 28 years earlier, whilst imprisoned in Genoa he had recounted his extraordinary adventures – a voyage stretching from the canals of Venice to the heart of the enigmatic Middle Kingdom – to fellow captive, romantic novelist Rustichello da Pisa. Whilst Rustichello is widely believed to have included some artistic licence, *The Travels of Marco Polo* became an overnight success.

Polo's narrative threw open the gates of an otherwise mystical Empire, giving Europeans their first comprehensive look into the inner workings of China. The stories depicted a realm of awe-inspiring immensity of enigmatic contrasts, where the ancient wisdom of Confucius and Taoism, long established in the nation's psyche, were the reigning doctrine. Confucianism is a symphony of ethical codes and societal principles, it's about creating a world as it should be, where personal virtues, social responsibilities, and familial bonds form a harmonious existence. Taoism, meanwhile, is more about living in harmony with the *Tao* or *The Way*. In medieval China, Taoist principles guided daily life, advocating for alignment with nature's rhythm instead of forcing outcomes.

Confucius, though long passed into the realm of immortality by the time of Marco Polo, was as alive as ever in the workplaces and grand palaces of China, influencing daily rituals, administrative stratagems, and even outlining the morals of the court. His teachings had become the basis for the Chinese bureaucracy, a system of examination and merit that bridged the divide between the ruler and the ruled, and a moral compass that guided the gentry and the peasant alike.

> *"Confucian texts contained a complicated theory of meritocracy: a theory that not only explained why society needed a caste of scholar-rulers to provide it with guidance but also how that elite should conduct itself from day to day, hour to hour"*[lvii]. – Adrian Wooldridge

For much of China's history, management of the empire was shared between the emperors "who inherited their authority by birth, and by professional scholar-officials, who attained their influence through their knowledge of Confucian doctrine"[lviii]. Marco Polo, arrived at the court of Kublai Khan, Great Khan of the Mongol Empire and ruler of China, who whilst an invader adopted many governing practices of his predecessors.

Centuries later another ruler, this time in France embraced this approach to their fledgling rule. Just as in the Imperial Court, Louis XIV centralised power in France. In a break from tradition, where the ministers of the King were plucked from the nobility and the church, Louis created and dispatched *intendants* a new category of royal officer, to oversee the provinces. Louis XIV "announced that he would henceforth govern alone, with no first minister. He surrounded himself with men selected not for their high birth, but instead for their abilities and loyalty"[lix]. The parallels with the Chinese practice of selecting highly-qualified scholars, based on rigorous examinations, to manage regional affairs and implement the emperor's vision is clear. Louis XIV had a deep affection for China, his private collection contained its art and he often sent emissaries to the Chinese. The fact that the first European translation of three of the four canonical books of Confucianism; the *Confucius Sinarum Philosophus* opens with a dedication to Louis XIV perhaps illustrates this influence best.

Marco Polo would go on to live in China for 17 years, travelling extensively and recalling stories of how the immense region was run through the bureaucratic might of the imperial court. An example of this can be read in Volume II of his book when he recounts the use of paper money – an alien concept for a European of the time.

> *"All these pieces of paper are issued with as much solemnity and authority as, if they were of pure gold or silver; and on every piece a variety of officials, whose duty it is, have to write their names, and to put their seals. And when all is prepared duly, the chief officer deputed by the Kaan smears the Seal entrusted to him with vermilion, and impresses it on the paper, so that the form of the Seal remains printed upon it in red; the Money is then authentic"*[lix] – Marco Polo.

Marco Polo's anecdote exemplifies the efficiency of the emperor's civil service. A multi-layered and effective state bureaucracy made up of the emperor's best subjects, not just those appointed from nepotism as was the norm in other parts of the world at this time. The mechanism to achieving this? The exam. As Socrates is purported to have said, "an unexamined human life is deprived of the meaning and purpose of existence". China took examination to a whole new level, inventing a new form of independent assessment as transformational as gunpowder, papermaking and the wheelbarrow.

The examination system was born during the Sui dynasty (581-618 CE) and with dynastic change evolved over the coming centuries to incorporate many of the approaches we'd recognise today, such as blind grading (copying a candidates' responses so that examiner would not be able to recognise their handwriting). Typically, candidates were put forward by their local prefecture and then examined by high officials. Each candidate was ranked on their 'talents and character', with the top performers being given jobs and opportunities for wealth and influence. The others were provided with more training. As Woodridge says, by the 'Tang dynasty examinations carried such prestige that even people who were eligible for hereditary office tried to pass them' [lxi]. Wooldridge humorously summarises the situation with direct historical contemporaries, "Imagine if Eric Bloodaxe had sat down to take an examination in order to rule Northumbria rather than relying on gore and pillage and you get a sense for how extraordinary this situation was". The civil service examinations were a stalwart of life in medieval China and continued right up into the modern era. China's first examination guide was devised in 1587, when Elizabeth I was on the throne of England and "might still have been in some use in 1905" [lxii].

The reason for the development of exams was multi-faceted. China is big, with "dozens of linguistic and ethnic groups with powerful regional traditions" [lxiii] and had a powerful elite of local lords and ruling bodies who had contended the authority of the emperor in the past. The examination system forced candidates with diverse regional roots to 'absorb a common classical idiom'. Demystifying diversity and getting everyone 'onto the same page', 'singing from the same hymn sheet', 'to fall in line, and 'see eye to eye'. Remarkable how many phrases have evolved in just the English language to warrant and value this approach. For the aristocracy, the effect of the examination system, and the power derived from passing it, 'persuaded local elites to focus their energies on providing their intellectual merits to the emperor rather than on establishing independent power bases' [lxiv].

The examination system was also a major draw for those not born into privilege. It provided one of the few, if not only, opportunities for those born into humble backgrounds (who could afford to devote themselves to studying), the chance to rise to dizzying heights of success. Wooldridge highlights how 'triumphant scholars erected memorial flagpoles or plaques outside their houses to proclaim their achievement to the world'.

In the context of workplaces, one of the enduring legacies of Confucius, who placed a high premium on education, the cultivation of morality, and the honing of practical skills, was the idea of meritocracy. For the rulers of Medieval China, the well-oiled machine of the imperial court was constantly fuelled and maintained by a ready supply of ambitious scholar-officials from across the empire. The system was so successful that its been adopted far and wide. Wooldridge cites French philosopher and historian Voltaire, who is said to have remarked, "The human mind cannot imagine a government better that this one where everything is to be decided by large tribunals, subordinated to each other, of which the members are received only after several severe examinations". In the United Kingdom, protestant missionaries brought back stories of how, 'In China, only talent, without the least respect to persons, is promoted…"[lxv]. The East India Company, founded in 1600 played a significant role in importing meritocratic ideology from the Far East. The cooperation adopted examinations to overcome the problem of "selecting able servants to administer a far-flung commercial empire"[lxvi]. In 1677, Samuel Pepys, the son of a tailor, introduced the first examinations for officers in the Royal Navy. Modernising the Royal Navy from a corrupt, inefficient force led by those born into privilege to an organised body led by those appointed on merit. An evolution the army would not experience for several more hundred years, much to its detriment.

The British Government found themselves caught in the revolutionary idea of examinations, seeing their undeniable worth in shaping civil service reforms. Victorian reformers Stafford Northcote and Charles Trevelyan asserted employment in the civil service was "eagerly sought after" by "the unambitious, and the dolent or incapable". In 1853, The Earl Granville proclaimed to the House of Lords, that 'one of the principle reasons why a small Tatar dynasty had governed the immense empire of China' was that it had secured the 'talent of the whole Chinese population by opening every official situation to competition'[lxvii]. Open competition was introduced in 1870 and a new class of elite civil servants were produced, who would soon earn a distinct moniker, a name resonating with their origin and still in common parlance if only satirically today – 'mandarins'.

Drawing from the Confucian ideals rooted in Medieval China, the concept of meritocracy—with its deep emphasis on continuous education and learning—has left its mark on various global systems, spanning from the dynastic courts of China, through Renaissance France, to the bureaucratic chambers of Victorian England. However, meritocracy extends beyond just selecting individuals for their innate merit; it's about cultivating and refining those talents through focused education and rigorous training.

Conversely, Taoism introduces a shift from structured curriculums towards embracing organic, unplanned learning experiences. Taoist educational thought notably challenges Confucian dogma, "the educational thought of Taoist also strongly dismisses the notion of 'learning', which is at odds with the Confucians and majority of Westerns"[lxviii]. Standing in contrast, the Taoist method centres on guiding or *teaching without words.*

In essence, while meritocracy champions the identification, nurturing, and advancement of talent, Taoism offers a counterpoint by challenging traditional educational frameworks. Both, however, hold crucial implications for modern workplace learning.

Japanese Mastery

Back with Marco Polo. Whilst living in China he was allegedly sent by the Emperor, Kublai Khan, on a diplomatic mission to Japan. In his memoirs, Marco Polo writes of the Japanese being ""well-mannered", "wholly independent", and "exercising no authority over any nation but themselves"[lxix] . There is some doubt as to whether he did reach the Japanese archipelago, but if he did, he would have encountered a nation very different to all he'd experienced to date. Onto Japan, the last destination in our circumnavigation of the medieval world.

Japan has always fascinated me, my Great Grandfather was the first British Ambassador to Japan in 1901 and whilst the majority of his collection including gifts from the emperor were donated to the Victoria and Albert Museum there are a few trinkets and artworks still in the family to captivate the imagination. They paint a picture, quite literally, of an alien world. A culture with a 265 year history of isolation, so different to almost everything else. But, we are not here to explore the evolution of their wonderful culture, and oh the food... but workplace learning.

We've briefly touched on the idea of *Takumi* – that it takes 60,000 hours to become a true master in your craft. Now we will explore their unique approach to craft mastery in more detail. The Japanese apprentice system is underpinned by a few key principles that differentiate it from Western vocational training programs.

Firstly, it is built on the concept of *learning by doing*. Apprentices are not mere educational receptacles; they actively participate in work alongside their mentors. They learn through direct hands-on experience, observing and mimicking their masters, gradually acquiring the skills and knowledge necessary for their trade through imitating, rather than being explicitly taught. They are given no explanation, it isn't the role of the apprentice to understand at this stage, just to copy. There is a Japanese term which explains this, *'gijutsu wo nusumu'* which can be translated as *'stealing the knowledge'*. This stage of the apprenticeship will last as long as it takes for the student to 'steal' the knowledge they need:

> *Rakugo is the 400-year-old traditional art of Japanese storytelling. There are two regional styles of the art form, the Kamigata style and the Tokyo style. The Kamigata version is practiced in western Japan and centers around the city of Osaka. The Tokyo version, as the name implies, is limited to the Kanto region, or eastern Japan. Kamigata rakugo practitioners engage in an apprenticeship lasting three years. Their counterparts in Tokyo endure an apprenticeship program which can last a grueling 15 years.* – Kristine Ohkubo[lxx]

Secondly, the relationship between master, the *'Shisho'* and apprentice is highly disciplined and marked by deep respect for both the master and the craft. Each apprentice goes on a structured journey to master their craft, but a different one to their European contemporaries. Instead of the regulated phases of Apprentice – Journeyman – Master, our Japanese apprentices would have experienced *Shu-Ha-Ri*.

ShuHaRi is a Japanese concept, describing the learning path to mastery and can be broken down as follows:

Shu, can be translated as *to keep, protect or maintain* and refers to the learning from tradition. Apprentices would emulate the work of their Shisho, making no modifications and not striving to comprehend the reasoning behind their mentor's teaching methods. An example I love can be seen in the dynamic between Daniel and Mr Miyagi in the film Karate Kid. Eager to learn the art of karate from the master, Mr Miyagi, Daniel is met with a condition: "First make sacred pact. I promise teach karate to you, you promise learn. I say, you do, no questions"[lxxi]. Upon accepting this pact, Daniel is instructed to "first wash all the car, then wax…" However, Daniel, puzzled about the relevance of this task to karate, interrupts. Mr Miyagi reminds him of their agreement and continues to demonstrate the desired technique: "wax on, wax off, breath, in through nose out through mouth, wax on, wax off, don't forget to breath. Very important"[lxxii]. It is only at a later point in the story that we discover that Daniel has indeed been receiving the training he so desired. Through the repetitive act of waxing on and off, he develops muscle memory as the movements become ingrained, a concept the Japanese refer to as *Kata*, or *the form*. **Shu** can be categorised as learning through observation, mimicking and repetition and results in a physical muscle memory and a mentality that fosters focus and concentration.

The stage of **Ha**, the next progression in the apprenticeship journey, is instigated by the Shisho, or master, rather than the apprentice. During the initial stage of **Shu**, the apprentice is akin to an empty vessel, filled gradually with the wisdom and expertise of the master. The term **Ha** can be interpreted quite literally as a process of *tearing up – an act of deep introspection, seeking novel methods, techniques, and wisdom*. When the apprentice reaches the stage of **Ha**, they are granted the freedom to question, to unshackle themselves from the strictures of tradition. At this stage, the apprentice must reflect on the meaning and purpose of who they are as well as their craft. As Mr Miyagi wisely said, "Lesson not just karate only. Lesson for whole life. Whole life have a balance. Everything be better"[lxxiii]. The stage of **Ha** nurtures individuality, enabling the student to blend their acquired knowledge with a profound comprehension of their own selves, their motivations, and the mechanisms that drive them. Essentially, **Ha** signifies the transition from being a passive recipient of knowledge to assuming proactive responsibility for one's personal growth.

The final stage of mastery Is **ri**, which can be understood as *separation, leave, to depart, release and set-free.* When an apprentice has reached this level they are no longer considered a student but as Arno Koch says, 'a pioneering practitioner'. The apprentice has now attained mastery having learnt the technical skills, knowledge and experience to produce original work in whatever craft they have chosen. As well as the self-reflection, understanding of oneself and ambition necessary to progress through the stages. *ShuHaRi* is not a linear path as we'd encounter in western apprenticeships, or certified like in China but a balance between Shu, Ha and Ri to create fully rounded masters. If you have the technical abilities but lack the introspection or drive you are not a master, the same can be said for the opposite, or as Mr Miyagi explains, "ambition without knowledge is like a boat on dry land."[lxxiv]

The Medieval period offers valuable insights for modern workplace learning strategies, with practices from different cultures around the world demonstrating a variety of effective methodologies.

In Europe, for example, the apprenticeship model and educational syllabus of the guilds emphasised rote learning. Where apprentices like John would learn their craft through continuous repetition and the subtleties of their profession through osmosis. Meanwhile, in China, the Confucian philosophy and use of examinations as a means of assessing excellence, laid the foundation for today's professional assessment.

The Islamic world during this period showcased blended learning, a combination of direct instruction and independent study as well as a licence to challenge contemporaries in the pursuit of better understanding. Finally, in Japan, the philosophy of continuous learning and introspection was highly valued. This mindset aligns with current views on lifelong learning in the workplace, emphasising the importance of continuous personal and professional growth.

The Medieval period, then, is not just a page in a dusty history book. It's a treasure trove of insights and ideas, a testament to the age-old quest for knowledge. And if we listen closely, it might just have a thing or two to teach us about learning in the modern workplace. And whilst as management consultant, Peter Drucker, says, "Knowledge is different from all other resources. It makes itself constantly obsolete, so that today's advanced knowledge is tomorrow's ignorance."[lxxv] The process by which we as humans learn does not change.

So, let's now move forward in time from the Medieval period in search of new evolutions in workplace learning practices.

Industrialisation

"What is learning? It is the ability to understand, to think, to act, to adapt, and to develop the human potential. It is the key to our survival in a changing world." Charles Handy

As we continue to trace the history of workplace learning, we find a significant shift occurring as we transition from the late Medieval age to the Industrial Revolution. The evolution of learning methods and practices to meet new demands of workers during this time laid the foundation for our modern understanding of workplace learning and employee development.

The craftsman of the late medieval period sought mastery in their craft. Their approach to achieving that as we have explored involved a mixture of different approaches to workplace learning and, in many cases, a lifelong embracing of it. Ensuring that apprentices gained not only technical expertise but also the tradecraft required to excel in their chosen profession.

However, as the world transitioned towards the industrial age, significant societal, economic, and technological changes impacted the nature of workplace learning. Greater levels of resources and commodities were needed to fuel the expansion of urban centres and demands from global trade. The craftsmen in their workshops could not keep up with demand, what was needed was sprawling factories, filled with workers, not seeing production through from start to finish as a craftsman might. But instead repeating a set action or task. The rise of new industries transformed the way people acquired skills and knowledge. This period witnessed a shift from individualised, mentor-based experiential-learning of craftsmen towards a more formal, structured approach to educate workers.

The trouble for industrialists with craftsmen is that they are expensive and difficult to replace. The mastery of their craft, which has taken years to acquire is simply so vast. Factory workers in comparison are much cheaper and far more expendable as a labour force. If you only need to teach a worker to master a tiny part of the process, not only can it be achieved faster but there are far more people who can do it. To answer this, need the Industrial Revolution saw the development of specialised institutions designed to educate specific trades and skills, such as mechanics institutes and technical schools. These institutions focused on providing practical, technical education akin to what they'd have experienced at school to prepare workers for the demands of the industrial workplace. The emphasis shifted from mastering a trade to knowing just enough specific, job-related skills.

Beyond education of the worker, the industrial age also saw the birth of scientific management principles and the heralding of a new actor, the middle manager. The writings of Frederick Winslow Taylor, the father of scientific management, emphasised the "need for efficiency, division of labor, and standardized training methods"[lxxvi]. This approach to workplace learning prioritised productivity and sought to create a workforce capable of adapting to the new industrial landscape through strict hierarchies and structured, replicable processes.

Whilst it's understandable to lament this new way of working, with focuses on human resource, middle management and task-orientated education. The evolution of workplace learning and development from the Industrial Revolution up until the Second World

War can be seen as a story of two contrasting tactics. On one hand, we do have the exploitation of workers, particularly children, in harsh working environments with minimal regard for their well-being. On the other hand, we have visionary business leaders who recognised the value of investing in their employees' well-being to drive productivity and profit.

The rise of the Industrial Revolution brought with it the need for a large, low-skilled workforce to keep up with the growing demand for goods and services. This led to the establishment of workhouses and factories, where men, women, and children were subjected to gruelling work conditions. Child labour was rampant, with young children forced to work long hours in hazardous environments, such as mines and textile mills. These children received little to no formal education or training, as their primary purpose was to serve as cheap labour for industries and there was little regard for their welfare so long as it didn't impose on the productivity of their workplace.

In stark contrast to this exploitative approach, some forward-thinking employers understood the connection between employee well-being and business success. Rowntree, the British confectionery company, was a pioneer in implementing employee welfare initiatives. The company's founder, Joseph Rowntree, believed that providing a safe, healthy, and supportive work environment would lead to happier, more productive employees, ultimately benefiting the business's bottom line.

Rowntree introduced a range of progressive measures to support employee learning and development, such as offering educational opportunities, investing in training programs, and providing facilities for leisure and recreation. The company's approach to workplace learning and development was rooted in the belief that investing in employee welfare would lead to increased loyalty, commitment, and productivity. A view shared by industrialist Henry Ford who supposedly said, "The only thing worse than training your employees and having them leave, is not training them, and having them stay".

As the years progressed towards the Second World War, there was a growing awareness of the need for improved working conditions and access to education for workers. Labour unions played a crucial role in advocating for better workplace learning and development opportunities, as well as fair wages and safer work environments. Governments also began to recognise the importance of investing in education and workforce development, leading to the establishment of public education systems and vocational training programs.

In summary, tracing the history of workplace learning from the late medieval age to the Industrial Revolution reveals the evolution of learning methods and practices that laid the foundation for today's understanding of workplace learning and development. While the medieval craftsman sought mastery in their trade, the industrial age brought about significant changes that transformed the way people learned and acquired skills. The shift from individualised, mentor-based learning to more formal, structured approaches prepared workers for the demands of the new industrial landscape.

During the industrial age, what was the essence of workplace learning underwent a major shift. What was historically, a hands-on, deeply personal journey between apprentice and master transformed into a more passive, uniform experience. The intimate one-on-one dynamic was overshadowed by a new 'one size fits all' approach, ushering in the advent of mass workforce education. Instead of workers taking the initiative to master their craft, the onus now lay with the employers. In order for the factories of the Industrial Revolution to function, employers needed to ensure their employees were equipped with the skills necessary for specific roles.

While the spotlight often shines on factory workers when discussing this transformative period, it's essential to understand that workplaces of all types underwent significant evolution. The era's drive for heightened productivity and efficiency gave birth to groundbreaking scientific management principles, and with them, the emergence of the middle manager.

But the implications ran deeper than just restructuring hierarchies and refining processes. These changes set the stage for our modern understanding of workplace learning. Reflecting on the journey from individual apprenticeships to broad mass-education provides clarity on today's emphasis on employee well-being, engagement, and the imperative of continuous growth. As the work landscape continues to evolve, these principles stand undiminished in their importance.

Globalisation

The 20th Century began tumultuously. The Industrial Revolution had supercharged the resource requirements of the European empires. Cartographers colour coded the new territories were carved out in every quadrant of the Globe. As different (mostly European) countries laid claim to the resources and people of newly created states, global maps resembled a patchwork quilt of colours, blues, pastels but notably not red, the colour traditionally associated with the British Empire. "Pink was a printer's compromise for letters overprinted to be clearly read"[lxxvii]. As the world was carved up and painted in the tension between European empires increased. But conflicts that had only decades earlier been largely confined to the European continent would now be played out on a global stage. The First and Second World Wars, arguably the most brutal and widespread conflicts in history, saw empires pitted against one another in battles of ideologies, territories, and resources.

However, as the curtains drew on the first half of the century, a transformational shift began to emerge. The scars of the wars, especially the devastation of the Second World War, inspired a collective yearning for peace. The globe, which had previously been a battleground of competing empires, began to weave a narrative of unity and cooperation. Nations, rather than vying for dominance, sought to intertwine their futures, driven by a mutual desire for prosperity and peace. Enter the rise of commercial confederacies. The European Union stands as a shining exemplar of this epoch, but it was far from alone. These alliances aimed to replace swords with ploughshares, or more aptly, with trade agreements and commercial ties. The underlying belief? Economic interdependence would be the antidote to conflict. After all, countries bound together by commerce would think twice before descending into disputes. Shared prosperity would act as both a shield and a balm, safeguarding nations from the cataclysms of wars and providing a framework for shared growth.

Yet, it would be remiss not to mention the remarkable technological innovations that sprouted from the soil of conflict. Wars, with their brutal urgency, spurred unprecedented advancements. But as the tides of war receded, these innovations didn't fade. Instead, they pivoted, driving the machinery of global commerce, bolstering communication, and shrinking the world in ways previously unimaginable. Technologies, such as 'The Collosus', the world's first programable digital computer, built in Britain to break encrypted messages from the German military, would go on to transform businesses. Similarly, the United States developed the ENIAC (Electronic Numerical Integrator and Computer), which was used to perform calculations for artillery firing tables. These early computers revolutionised computing and paved the way for the post-war digital age. These developments not only influenced the outcome of the war but contributed to the transition of workers from factories to offices.

The post-war years saw companies focusing on growth and prosperity to rebuild their nations. Employees who had previously been little more than human machines were increasingly viewed as valuable assets that contributed to the rebuilding process. As a result, businesses invested in their workforce by providing opportunities for learning and development. On-the-job training became a common method of equipping employees with the skills necessary for their roles, whilst the office itself provided the effective environment for experiential learning of their tradecraft. As the decades passed and technology advanced, the nature of work began to change dramatically. The rise of computers heralded the rise of knowledge-based roles. The competitive advantage of an educated workforce became increasingly evident, prompting businesses to prioritise employee development. Educational institutions expanded their offerings, and third party vocational training programs emerged to meet the growing demand for skilled workers in specialised industries with standardised education, assessment and certification. Similar to the apprentice guilds of medieval times.

In Germany, the focus on technical and vocational training helped maintain a highly skilled workforce. The German dual system, which combines classroom learning with on-the-job training, ensured that employees received both theoretical education and practical experience. This approach has arguably contributed to the success of German manufacturing and engineering companies, such as Siemens and BMW in the wake of the war.

In Japan, the post-war period was characterised by demilitarisation and the rebuilding of the nation's economy. Rapid transformation led to the emergence of a technology-driven, office-based economy, with corporations such as Toyota and Honda at the forefront. As the nature of work shifted, so did the approaches to employee learning and development as they transitioned from purely educating employees for specialist task needs to a broader, more holistic form of continuous improvement. This different approach to employee development, laid the foundation for the concept of "kaizen".

Kaizen, means *"change for the better"*. And emphasises continuous improvement and learning in the workplace, encouraging employees to contribute ideas and actively participate in the company's growth. This culture of learning and development significantly contributed to Japan's competitive edge in the global market. As Masaaki Imai, author of "Kaizen: The Key to Japan's Competitive Success" said, "In post-war Japan, the concept of 'kaizen' or continuous improvement became the cornerstone of Japan's recovery and subsequent economic success. This approach to business and industry has driven Japan to become a global economic powerhouse."[lxxviii]

Similar trends emerged in the United States, where the workforce transitioned from manufacturing industries to the knowledge economy. As companies like IBM, Xerox, and Microsoft began to shape the technological landscape, the nature of work moved from hands-on skills to knowledge-based roles. Consequently, American corporations started investing heavily in employee education and development to keep up with the ever-changing technological demands. IBM, for example, created the IBM Systems Research Institute in 1960 to provide advanced technical training for its employees. Xerox, on the other hand, established the Xerox Learning Systems in the 1970s to deliver training and development programs for its workforce. At the same time, Motorola a company established in Chicago at the turn of the century established the Motorola University, offering in-house training to improve employees' technical skills. This led to the development of Six Sigma, a system of techniques and tools for process improvement, which has since become widely adopted.

The transition from factories to offices brought about a profound impact on employee learning and development. Office environments necessitated skilled workers in knowledge-based roles, leading to a greater emphasis on continuous learning and upskilling. Companies worldwide began to invest in employee development programs, recognising the importance of keeping their workforce up-to-date with the latest technologies and industry trends. This shift led to the rise of Learning Management Systems (LMS), in-house training programs, and collaborations with educational institutions. An LMS could bring the content to your employees rather than have them head out for the local night school or community college. The UK's Open University was an early adopter of the original LMS system called firstClass, which was a Canadian product. The LMS idea was exactly what companies were looking for at the time – a place where employees could access material at any point from their work stations and there were management options that let human resources and other higher-ups see who was doing what, what had been completed, and how well the employees were taking to the content. As time moved on, however, LMS became less and less about actual learning, and more and more about assigning educational tasks that needed to be completed to keep up with corporate mandates and compliance needs. It went from a tool with a great potential to a way to ensure that the bare minimum needs for the company to stay on the right side of the letter of the law were being met.

Ever since there was a need for workplace regulation, compliance training had been a part of learning and development. But it was in the late 20th Century, that the regulatory landscape for businesses transformed. During this period, governments across the globe introduced new legislation, such as the United Kingdom's, 'Health and Safety at Work etc. Act' (1974) and the established new government bodies such as 'The Occupational Safety and Health Administration' (1971) in the USA to protect employee rights, ensure workplace safety, and maintain ethical business practices. Ensuring that employees were aware of the ever growing and increasingly complex workplace regulations fell on the shoulders of the learning and development practitioners.

Globalisation took on a whole new momentum from the late 20th century. The end of the Cold War in the 1990s enshrined the USA's position as the sole-superpower and with it the doctrine of democracy and free market economies. The philosophical victors over communism and isolationism. This paved the way for multi-national companies to rise and take advantage of newly minted democracies and the liberalisation of their trade. In 1995, the World Trade Organisation ("WTO") was created with the goal of reducing trade barriers and promoting economic integration. In 1993, the European Union launched the single market. Establishing four freedoms of movement of people, goods, services and money. As the European Union website highlights, with these developments, "Hundreds of laws have been agreed since 1986 covering tax policy, business regulations, professional qualifications and other barriers to open frontiers" [lxxix] . The education of all of these new regulations had to be passed onto employees.

In 2008, the financial crisis had a major effect on compliance training and led to a renewed emphasis on the importance of training employees to adhere to regulatory and ethical practices. As businesses faced more scrutiny from regulators and government agencies, employers double downed their investment in compliance training. Ostensibly to better ensure that their employees were better equipped to navigate the new regulations in the pursuit of their daily work. But, it should also be recognised that this investment was driven by a fear of pecuniary penalty and reputational loss.

In 2012, HSBC agreed to pay a record fine of $1.9 billion to United States authorities to settle allegations of money laundering and sanction violations. The then United States Assistant Attorney General, Lanny A. Breur said of this case, "HSBC is being held accountable for stunning failures of oversight – and worse – that led the bank to permit narcotics traffickers and others to launder hundreds of millions of dollars through

HSBC subsidiaries, and to facilitate hundreds of millions more in transactions with sanctioned countries". The quote highlights a general theme in the report that led to the fine being paid, that HSBC had not provided sufficient compliance training to their employees. In this case, resulting in a severe financial penalty. Another case, this time in the UK was that of Standard Chartered Bank in 2014, when they were fined £102 million by the Financial Conduct Authority (FCA) for anti-money laundering breach. Similarly, the bank was accused of failing to establish and maintain appropriate risk sensitive policies and procedures, leading to insufficient training for its employees in the area of AML compliance. At the time Standard Chartered Bank accepted the findings and the "second largest financial penalty ever"[lxxx].

This period is interesting for workplace learning as a notable evolution in purpose and strategy emerges. No longer was it just about equipping employees with job skills as in the period of the Industrial Revolution, but now to also do them compliantly. And how to ensure and document workforce understanding? Examinations. As in the Mandarin Court, workers around the world would now be routinely tested. Compliance training, now a two-pronged tool, serves as both a shield against potential legal pitfalls and a swift response in crisis situations. Faced with a dilemma, should workplace learning primarily be a protective measure or a catalyst for personal growth? With the dawn of the 2020s and the advent of the coronavirus pandemic, this balance became even more pivotal, transforming workplace learning from a mere skill booster to an indispensable element of risk management.

Covid19

"The pandemic has revolutionized corporate learning." – Fortune Magazine. (2021)

A s we've seen throughout history, it takes a cataclysm that affects large swathes of the population and how the world functions for things to undergo significant change. This notion became strikingly evident with the onset of the 2020, coronavirus pandemic. Covid, would go on to claim over five million lives around the world and affect billions more. The pandemic's far-reaching impact on public health, economies, jobs, mental health, education, and daily routines have been substantial. It would be immensely challenging to find a single person on earth who has not experienced some degree of change or disruption due to the pandemic. For that reason, the pandemic and its effects on learning and development requires a chapter of its own.

I still remember the day I first heard of coronavirus vividly. I was in the bustling city of Mumbai, a delegate on a UK government trade mission. The city was alive with its usual vibrancy, a cacophony of honking horns, busy people, and the ceaseless hum of a city alive. Our days were a whirlwind of activity - meetings, tours, networking events - each moment filled with the promise of new connections and opportunities.

Someone had been briefed us about this emerging virus in China. But, to me at least, it was something distant, a whisper of unease that seemed far removed from the immediacy of our mission. Extra precautions were to be taken, we were told. Hand sanitisers started appearing everywhere, masks, once a rare sight, became a common accessory. The people we met, once so quick to extend a hand in greeting, began to hesitate. Some asked not to shake hands, their polite smiles not quite reaching their eyes. Others requested we maintain a certain distance, their voices apologetic yet firm – admittedly, I wrote this off as hypercautious. Little did I know that in just a matter of weeks it would become government policy.

In the workplace, the impact of coronavirus and particularly the measures taken around the world to mitigate the spread of the virus were profound. As the pandemic unfolded, the global economy was further challenged by dwindling profit margins and a surge in bankruptcies, prompting a significant transformation in multiple sectors of the often-impersonal business world. Corporate leaders began to place a higher emphasis on employee well-being, with their concern manifesting in the decisions they made. This shift, influenced by a blend of responsibility and empathy, was spurred by the "shared challenges encountered by leaders and employees alike during the COVID-19 pandemic"[lxxxi]. The pandemic-induced lockdowns functioned as a unifying factor across the socioeconomic spectrum, as people irrespective of *who they were,* were confined to their homes. The concerns of often overlooked employee demographics, including single parents and older people, emerged as focal points for employers who were suddenly able to relate like never before. Whilst in part a duty of care there was an element of real empathy that shone through in many businesses. I think a lot of this had to do with the simple fact that the business owners and leaders were suddenly in the same situation as their employees.

The average salary for a FTSE100 CEO is one hundred and three times (£3.4m) the average UK salary. Unsurprisingly therefore, this connection doesn't happen all too much because usually being rich and powerful allows you to rise above the more common problems that most people suffer, like inflation and economic downturns. No matter how wealthy you were during the COVID-19 pandemic, you were still locked down at home like everyone else, waiting impatiently for a cure like everyone else, and getting incessantly frustrated that you couldn't go visit loved ones, take a holiday, or get back to your office to see your colleagues like you wanted to.

The pandemic precipitated a transformation in the realm of employee learning and development. As everything that could be, was shifted online, businesses had to embrace innovative education technology ("edtech") solutions "resulting in a growing reliance on online platforms for learning, content delivery, collaboration, conferences, and one-on-one meetings"[lxxxii] to maintain productivity and ensure continuity of employee education. Whilst pre-pandemic only a few had experienced video calls on online conferencing platforms almost all of us are now familiar with Zoom, Google Meets and Microsoft Teams. For Zoom, daily users went from 10 million in December 2019, to 350 million just one year later.

This isn't to say that pre-pandemic edtech was non-existent. In fact, the earliest form of edtech can be assigned to the invention of the printing press by Johannes Gutenberg in the 15th century. The opportunity to print books revolutionised the dissemination of information. Making knowledge transfer increasingly accessible. Knowledge transfer is largely what education technology has been used for. In the 20th century, radio and later television gave power to the authorities to broadcast educational content. In many cases this new form of content delivery was used for good with an educational content focusing on a range of topics from agriculture to foreign languages. The UK's, Open University, leveraged the growing ownership of television sets in the 1970s to provide education to people unable to attend traditional institutions. Stalwarts of children's television were also introduced during this time, Mr Rogers, Sesame Street and the Electric Company. Of his approach to children's education, Fred Rogers said, "Play is often talked about as if it were a relief from serious learning. But for children, play is serious learning".

However, the ability to educate people *en masse* contributed to several authoritarian regimes amassing power often democratically. The rise of the Nazi party in 1930s Germany has often been attributed to the radio, as Rentschler highlights, "By 1941 65% of German households owned a [Government made radio]"[lxxxiii]. A poignant reminder even today to always consider who is doing the education.

In the 1980s-90s personal computers followed in the footsteps of radio and television providing innovative new solutions for knowledge transfer. New software programs like The Oregon Trail and Reader Rabbit targeted young learners with a fun and engaging user experience, showing how technology could make learning more enjoyable. The rise of the internet in the late 1990s and early 2000s made an even bigger impact. As universities began offering their courses online a new market was created by edtech entrepreneurs. Content libraries and Massive Open Online Courses ("MOOCs") from organisations like Lynda (later to become LinkedIn Learning) Coursera and edX. These vast online libraries made high-quality education available to anyone with an internet connection, regardless of where they lived.

In concert with the growth of content libraries were Learning Management Systems, ("LMSs") used by businesses to facilitate course delivery for their people as well as tracking employee progress. As technology evolved the complexity and range of feature of LMS systems like, Blackboard, Moodle and TalentLMS increased.

Of course, we fell into the austere, disconnected trap during the COVID-19 pandemic because it was the only solution we had. We had to work from home, and thankfully technology allowed us to still do a lot of good in the world despite being all over the map. But the more time we spent apart, the more time we started losing on the connective tissue of both learning and community. We were no longer learning from our co-workers, other than what one room in their homes looked like on the daily Zoom calls. When we allowed people to keep working from home when the all clear calls started to be made, we were allowing people to do what was easy instead of what was right. "There was a fundamental element missing, which is - what are we really trying to achieve," says LHH's Dr Burak Koyuncu. "We got fixated on technical skills of what you want to know. In the training, we focused on the non-people element and we forgot the key element of reflecting, applying our knowledge together, and connecting with them and learning from them."

Clearly, the pandemic did not trigger the invention of edtech but it did create an environment where businesses who have never touched anything digital were forced to adopt it. But, it did dismantle established norms and presented a conundrum for employers. Learning and development programmes that had typically been provided in person, with instructor-led training or conference style workshops were shoe-horned into digital formats. An easier proposition for those already familiar with LMSs and content libraries but not necessarily any easier for the employees. Udemy, an edtech company that provides online learning to individuals and businesses released a report in 2020, highlighting the surge in user registration. The report said, "In a month, [Udemy] saw 425% enrolment growth from individuals, an 80% increase in use by businesses and governments, and 55% growth in new course creation" [lxxxiv]. There is a clear corelation between lockdowns being announced by governments around the world and users in those countries joining the platform. Coursera, another edtech solution had 10 million new user enrolments, up 640%, in a 30-day period starting in mid-March. The same time that then Prime Minister Boris Johnson announced the first lockdown in the United Kingdom, ordering people to "stay at home".

However, a significant obstacle emerged in this new landscape of remote work and learning. Simply put, joining is not synonymous with engaging. Engagement refers to the "extent to which [learners] are engaging linked with high-quality learning outcome" [lxxxv]. While digital solutions made it feasible to deliver education and training remotely, maintaining user engagement proved to be a more formidable challenge. This was particularly true given the increased screen time that remote work necessitated.

Compliance training, development programmes, and even individual coaching found themselves vying for employee attention amidst a myriad of other business activities. For the first time, all these different facets of work and learning were competing within the same medium - the digital screen. This presented a unique challenge for practitioners who had invested considerable time and effort into creating the best courses or programmes that remote work would allow.

Despite the meticulous planning and preparation, the level of engagement ultimately rested in the hands of the employees. They were the ones who had to decide how much they could afford to prioritise their engagement with these learning opportunities over their other work responsibilities. This reality was starkly reflected in the completion rates of online courses, which often fell short of expectations.

As our existence became increasingly tethered to the glowing screens of our digital devices' problems arose. Constant exposure to the computer-generated world exacerbated 'digital fatigue', a consequence of our utter reliance upon smart phones and Zoom calls for our social and commercial interaction. Employees around the world found themselves under siege from the relentlessness of round-the-clock connectivity. At the height of lockdown, Professor Timothy Hoff released a study on Covid's effect on professionals and work, he said, "the pandemic has forced adaptations that foment values and psychological states including self-preservation, resilience, optimism, courage, compassion, self-esteem, burnout, citizenship, and self-efficacy"[lxxxvi]. For many, this virtual fatigue was magnified by the pervasive sense of social isolation and anxiety that had become the zeitgeist of the period. Simultaneously, a more covert adversary emerged. The once clear demarcation between professional and personal lives became ambiguous. The sudden shift to remote work blurred traditional boundaries as the rhythm of daily commutes, office banter, and even professional attire got washed away in the tidal wave of home-bound work.

The loss of the office, the biosphere for company culture, processes, systems, and work relationships had additional consequences for workplace learning. Even if employees weren't interested in taking courses or using their LMS, they were still picking up a lot of skills via osmosis; seeing other people succeed with certain approaches and picking up the nuances of colleagues and line managers along the way. As Dr Burak Koyuncu, LHH's head of Leadership Development told me, "Learning is not an activity that you do in isolation. It needs to be part of the culture of the organisation. It needs to be part of the way of working". For employees, it wasn't just figuring out how to get work email on phones or where to find policy X or Y either, but subtle things like how to talk with customers, reflecting on a meeting with a colleague as you walk back to your desk or even troubleshooting obstacles at the water cooler. These things didn't have to be explicitly taught when employees saw them play out and were able to subconsciously reflect on them every day.

"In a virtual world, we behave in a much different way than we do in person, we don't even think about it, though. When we're in the office and we leave a meeting, we walk back to our stations talking with each other about what we heard, what we think, and what we're going to do about it. What do you do when you don't walk to meetings anymore because you're just hitting the 'leave' button? Young employees are no longer getting the osmosis of learning from older employees. If I only have a relationship with you virtually, it's hard to really know you." – Steve Margison

The pandemic undeniably threw a spanner in the workplace engine. But not all of it was bad. New environments change behaviours. What I mean by this is that when you remove the office 'environment', you lose the herd mentality. As the context of work changes so too do conventional behaviours. Because of this, disruption and chaos, as jarring and uncomfortable as they may be, have historically served as powerful catalysts for innovation and opportunity. 'Resilience' was the common message from Governments. What I found interesting was that the term resilience has its roots in Latin, derived from "*resilio*", which actually translates to "*rebound*". Examples of rebounding from crisis are common throughout history. Since we haven't yet looked at Ancient Rome, let's pluck an example from 24 BC when a great fire decimated the metropolis. Rome rebounded from disaster and constructed the Aqua Virgo. This was a collosal aqueduct aimed to curb any future threat of fire. Not only did this innovation fortify Rome's water supply, it also cemented the groundwork for future sophisticated water management systems around the world. Indeed, the treatise, *De architectura* written at the time by architect, Marcus Vitruvius "has become a principal guide and a revered text, and has influenced architects from the Renaissance to the present day"[lxxxvii]. A more recent example is the Fukushima nuclear disaster in

2011, when a tsunami triggered by a major earthquake caused three of Fukushima's four reactors to meltdown. Due to radioactive releases, 100,000 people were evacuated from their homes, (as of 2023, many are still yet to return). The disaster had a profound effect on the public perception of nuclear energy, and "led to a ~4% growth in global renewable energy generation" [lxxxviii]. Upheavals, however terrible, spur radical progress and bring forth new paradigms.

You're in an environment where there is no map, it's completely open ended. Within workplaces, there is an adaptive resilience that necessitates creativity and unified effort. Margison says, "Nobody knows how to do these things. You're inventing the technology; you're inventing the paradigms and the ways of thinking. So, you become very agile, inclusive. You share ideas. You think much more". Suddenly, doors that had previously been obstacles, or paths that had been obfuscated were flung open. Margison goes on to recount what a virologist involved in the flu vaccine said about it;

"So it's terrible, but it's also the most exciting period of my career ever. Because, suddenly all of these competitive academics from around the world who couldn't speak to each other before, because they're all quite protective, are working together. And we've made more advances in virology in months that we've made in decades." – Anonymous

Without the confines of uniformity individualism flourishes. In its physical manifestation, business attire went from neutral office wear to hoodies and sweatpants. Employees could create their own environments, with their own rules. Nobody was going to judge them eating an egg and cress sandwich at their desk or playing Duran Duran's *Hungry Like the Wolf* at full volume before each sales call. Employees were able to disengage from the identity of being just another 'brick in the wall' down at the corporate headquarters because suddenly they weren't at corporate headquarters anymore. They weren't the lady in the third cubicle on the fifth row opposite the break room; they were now Isabella, the remote-working super mum who was starting to realise she didn't want to be a widget salesperson after all. Maybe what she really wanted was to be artistic and creative and if her company couldn't provide her that sort of opportunity, well she was going to pull the plug on the whole thing and venture out on her own... and many did just that.

In May 2021, Anthony Klotz, a professor of business administration at Texas A&M University, coined the 'Great Resignation' to explain the extraordinary rate at which employees were resigning from their jobs as Covid uncertainty stabilised. Klotz explained that, "The numbers are multiplied, by the many pandemic-related epiphanies—about family time, remote work, commuting, passion projects, life and death, and what it all means—that can make people turn their back on the 9-to-5 office grind"[lxxxix]. According to a survey by the Pew Research Centre, "one-in-five non-retired U.S. adults (19%) – including similar shares of men (18%) and women (20%) – say they quit a job at some point in 2021, meaning they left by choice and not because they were fired, laid off or because a temporary job had ended"[xc]. Whilst the most common reasons given for quitting were low pay and a lack of advancement opportunities, we should also factor in "pandemic experiences led some workers to revaluate life priorities and reduce working hours or leave the labor force entirely"[xci].

As the Great Resignation continued employers had to compete for talent, "with the full array of work experiences available to today's employees—traditional and nontraditional (gig work or part-time) jobs and, in some instances, not working at all"[xcii]. The dynamic shifted, employers no longer held all the cards and could make all the rules. They recognised that in order to secure the expertise they wanted they'd need to offer more than remuneration incentives. They were necessitated to recognise that most of the workforce wanted workplace flexibility, development opportunities, and a meaningful culture [xciii]. A sense of belonging, a community.

The real difficulty for employers now was how to provide these simultaneously. The mass-acceptance of workplace flexibility or hybrid working as it has become known means that the office will never again be the learning fulcrum it once was. It's not just a sense of freedom and a dissipation of corporate culture going on here, either. The people who are going to seek out new ways to improve themselves are already watching TED talks and earning credits at Coursera. It's the ones that need a guiding hand to drive them towards learning objectives that are now even farther from that sort of objective than ever. The office experience has been diluted and it is unlikely that it will ever return to what it once was. A recent survey by Knight Frank, found "about half of large multinationals are planning to cut office space in the next three years as they adapt to the rise of homeworking since the coronavirus pandemic." [xciv] Consequently, at any point only a percentage of your workforce can physically be present at any given time. This understandably causes concern for employers who now recognise the spontaneously-generated cultural mecca that the office environment was. Patrick Dunne recalls a meeting where this was discussed, "So, with less space you have to make a decision on which third of the people to have back. And the decision, which I thought was really clever, was to have the older, wiser mentor group and the really young ones and the middle ones were kind of working from home". The employee who used to rely on their cubicle mate to help them understand all the new technology no longer has that choice. Even with the 30-second conversation at the water cooler three times a week, a line manager could establish a general sense of rapport with his or her subordinates. Now that was reduced to Zoom calls every Monday morning where some people had the video off, some people lagged through the whole meeting, and some did everything they could to avoid speaking a single syllable. "The pandemic didn't create problems, it revealed problems that were already there," says HRM Professor Roberta Sawatzky. "If a team couldn't communicate well, it wasn't because of the pandemic, it was because when they were in person before COVID they also couldn't communicate well. The pandemic just revealed all of their crutches." Sawatzky touches on a bitter truth, even when we were in our offices, we often failed to get it right.

The Coronavirus pandemic has had lasting implications on the workplace, the workers and how employers' foster learning and instil education. Amidst the chaos and uncertainty, leaders had licence to try new things without fear of reprimand. The context changed, and with-it behaviours. The carefully cultivated biospheres of corporate life have been challenged by the expectations of work-flexibility and individualism. The shift has not been without its trials, its losers and its winners. Employers have had to adapt, and will need to continue doing so in order to ensure that their workforce can execute their business strategies and goals. Either way, it was a cataclysmic event and may perhaps serve as the opportunity we've needed, to break free from the shackles of what workplace learning became and consider now what it could become.

But first, back to our Dickensian plan, we will be visited by the ghost of 'workplace learning present'. To explore workplace learning's two most puissant forces; employers and employees. These independent entities coexist, yet these symbionts often find themselves in a state of palpable tension, an adversarial position that sometimes even extends beyond mere intellectual disagreements.

Part 2. The Tectonic Struggle of Workplace Learning

"You don't learn to walk by following the rules. You learn by doing and falling over" - Sir Richard Branson

A t the crux of workplace learning exist two principal actors; employers and employees, embroiled in a tectonic struggle. Less good and bad or darkness and light. More a rock and a hard place.

This is not a new struggle but an intrinsic aspect of the employer-employee relationship since the dawn of organised work. Throughout history, this dynamic has been a crucible for both conflict and collaboration, with each side seeking to fulfil its needs and desires. As societal values and market conditions evolve, the struggle continuously morphs, and with it, so do the strategies employed by both employers and employees to get what they want and need.

Employers face the daunting challenge of anticipating future skill requirements and cultivating a workforce equipped to thrive in an uncertain future. Simultaneously, employees must navigate the complex terrain of career and personal development, honing their skills and abilities to remain relevant and competitive.

In this part of the book, we will delve deeper into the various aspects of this tectonic struggle, exploring the diverse perspectives and strategies employed by both employers and employees in their ongoing quest for growth and success in the realm of workplace learning and development. How new technologies, social attitudes and demands for evaluation are shaping learning in today's workplaces. Then we will culminate by exploring the mission, aspirations and challenges of the practitioners, the learning leaders who shoulder the burden of uniting these two stakeholders behind common learning goals and initiatives.

ii. The Needs of Employers

"I've learned that people will forget what you said, people will forget what you did, but people will never forget how you made them feel." – Maya Angelou

L et's first examine the employer stakeholder. As we discovered in the previous part on the history of learning, technological innovations, globalisation, and changing working practices have all affected the role of education and learning in organisations. From the experiential relationship between craftsmen and their apprentices to the Industrial Revolution where training became more task-focused, and the computer age where the scope of Learning and Development was broadened. Workplace learning has come a long way. But what exactly do employers need from their L&D programs today?

We've already clarified that the purpose of Learning and Development is to help employers execute strategy. But what does this mean in practice? In general, employers are seeking effectiveness and value (or return on investment) from their L&D programs. It's important to note however that not every expectation we cover will be a top priority for every employer. Individual circumstances will dictate where the focus lies, but this is a comprehensive list of what I believe to be on the employer's "wish list" when it comes to their L&D.

We will start with effectiveness. Whilst employers do of course want all of their initiatives to be effective, this refers to ensuring that an employer's learning and development program guarantees their people have what they need to do their job.

From onboarding new employees to developing existing talent. Learning and Development is tasked with making sure that people have the skills and knowledge they need to execute effectively. This naturally includes both technical skills and soft skills, that are essential for an employee to perform their job responsibilities. An example of this in practice comes from Unilever, a multinational consumer goods company. Their L&D programme, *'Unilever Future Leaders Programme'* (UFLP), focuses on developing leadership capabilities and industry-specific skills through immersive experiences and real-life challenges. As Alan Jope, Unilever's CEO, states, "The UFLP is designed to equip our future leaders with the skills and knowledge necessary to succeed in today's competitive market". Jope's quote reads well, you can probably imagine it as a closing soundbite for the AGM, but what does it actually mean for an employer's workplace learning programme? What are the *skills and knowledge necessary to succeed*, and who is responsible for identifying them?

Identifying what an employers' people need in order to be effective has been a significant challenge for employers throughout history. But never have we experienced such rapid technological advancement and evolution in workplace practices. Each new paradigm requires a different assortment of skills in order for employees to thrive. For example, if in an effort to lure talent an employer is now offering flexible working, then there is little point in putting those employees through training that is predicated on the assumption that they will all be back in the office. Margison explains, "as long as we exist in a virtual world, then the tradecraft skills you need are about being able to exist in a virtual world".

The traditional understanding of necessary workplace competencies is being further assailed by new technologies. The release of OpenAI's Generative Predictive Text models in early 2023 heralded a turning point in general purpose artificial intelligence. What can take an author, coder, designer days, weeks even months to generate, the GPT models can do in a matter of seconds. For now, the models' outputs are not quite at human standard (as much as I wish it could, it can't write a book), OpenAI admits as much, "the model still has important limitations. It can produce plausible-sounding but incorrect responses" [xcv]. Nevertheless, the models will undoubtedly improve and combined with the efficiency of artificial intelligence, they are going to have a profound impact on workplace skills.

The World Economic Forum (WEF) have recently forecasted a seismic shift in workplace skills. They believe that nearly a quarter of all jobs will be disrupted by AI over the next five years[xcvi]. The skills most at risk from this technological revolution are, ironically, those that have long been considered stalwarts of the workplace. According to the OECD's Centre for Educational Research and Innovation, "70% of workers use literary skills everyday… 50% of workers perform numeracy tasks daily at work"[xcvii].

This presents employers with a strategic conundrum. Should they invest in training their workforce to use these AI systems, effectively integrating the technology into their existing operations? Or should they replace roles entirely, ceding ground to the machines? Then again, employers could focus on nurturing the skills that AI can't *currently* replicate, those uniquely human qualities.

Certainly, according to the WEF report on jobs, the skills that are growing in importance most rapidly are socio-emotional. Skills such as "lifelong learning; resilience, flexibility and agility; and motivation and self-awareness" [xcviii]. Yuval Noah Harari, author of *Sapiens: A brief history of humankind* explained this, "Most important of all will be the ability to deal with change, to learn new things and to preserve your mental balance in unfamiliar situations. In order to keep up with the world of 2050, you will need not merely to invest new ideas and products – you will above all need to reinvent yourself again and again". Evidence, perhaps, that businesses are embracing a strategy that cultivates a resilient workforce and a culture of lifelong learning. Whilst these human qualities are at the top of the list, 'systems thinking, AI and big data' are in the top 10. With so much flux the principal challenge for employers is in deciding their strategy, but as Jonathan Eighteen from Deloitte recognises that presents a significant challenge.

"Job architectures are getting thrown up in the air. Consequently, it's crucial to strategise around this new landscape. A key part of this involves assessing the skills we currently have and identifying those we need. However, navigating this process is a complex challenge." – J. Eighteen

In the late medieval period, technological innovation occurred, but at a much slower pace than today. The gradual speed of change made it comparatively easier to assess what skills were needed and how to train people up. This gave employers ample time to adjust and to remain competitive. In most cases an employee would have a set 'path' for their career, established and structured long before they commenced their employment.

This only really began to change in the late 18th century with the technological advancements of the Industrial Revolution. This era marked a significant shift in societal structures and practices, as new technologies were harnessed to revolutionise production processes. The primary objective was simple yet powerful: to produce more, faster. The potential for significant wealth generation motivated a new class of society, the industrialist, whose burgeoning influence would change the social fabric itself.

But, this period of rapid change and progress was not universally welcomed. In England, the Luddite movement emerged as a potent symbol of resistance. Luddites were often skilled craftsman who saw their livelihoods threatened by the introduction of machines. Their skills, honed over a lifetime or apprenticeship, practice and reflection were suddenly in danger of becoming obsolete, replaced by machines that could do their work faster, 24/7 and cheaper.

In response to these concerns, the luddites embarked on a campaign of physical protest. They targeted the very symbols of their displacement - the machines - and set about destroying them. They even invented a leader, Ned Ludd who purposefully bore an uncanny resemblance to another folk hero of the oppressed, Robin Hood. Indeed, the Luddites went so far as to create a fictitious office for their invented leader, from where they would send letters that spread panic among the British authorities and industrialists. These letters signed by "Mr Ludd's Office, Sherwood Forest", served to further entrench the image of the Luddites as modern-day social-justice warriors.

Today we find ourselves in the midst of another technological revolution. This time, it's not mechanised looms but artificial intelligence and automation that are causing concern. Just as the Luddites feared the loss of their traditional livelihoods, many workers today worry about the impact of AI on their jobs. In France, work stoppages were called in protest of Amazon increasingly automating its warehouses. In the USA, the Writers Guild of America have called the largest strike in over a decade, concerned by online streaming and AI.

Yet the march of technological progress endures. And, is likely to continue to do so. Robert Solow, a Nobel Laureate of Economics, developed a theory on growth that analyses the level of output or productivity over time. The model amongst a variety of other things, highlights that only through technological progress can permanent growth be achieved.

For employers, Solow's model implies that technological progress is not only inevitable but also a crucial driver of productivity and growth – perhaps the primary motivator for any business. As such, employers must develop strategies that both harness technology and prepare and adapt their people.

Pretty straightforward in the cold efficiency of industrial age factories. Where workers assigned a station, where they would repeat an often-simple sequence of actions made the identification and training of skills simpler. For these workers, the training process used was 'Rote Learning', effectively teaching through repetition. Rote learning has been around since ancient times, where the ability to regurgitate knowledge was greatly valued in a largely illiterate world. Workers with specific tasks were taught in this way, and there is little coincidence that the birth of modern schooling originated at this time with a similar approach. And, it certainly works. I had one teacher, who each year ran a rote-learning programme. It happened in the second month, and a quota was kept of every time one of his pupils misspelt, *February*. The offender would have to rewrite the word, the number of times doubling in a geometric sequence.

Whilst having its merits for the efficient transmission of knowledge for factory workers, children and the month of February. Rote learning's rigid nature was less effective for other workforce skills that required critical thinking and creativity. Essential components of any business. Its rigidity fell short in cultivating skills demanding creativity and critical thinking—core tenets of any thriving business. As the race to leverage new technologies heated up, employers yearned for innovative minds. Yet, the mainstream learning and development landscape largely sidestepped soft skills, placing emphasis on technical competencies, like machinery operation. While technical schools and work training sessions honed vocational talents, the nurturing of soft skills was often left to individual initiative, subtly shaped by workplace interactions and social dynamics.

When it came to soft skills employers were able to identify what they needed, but that onus for its development was on the employee. Not the employer. Andrew Carnegie, amongst the wealthiest industrialists of this age exemplified this belief that employees should 'fit the mould', said, "People who are unable to motivate themselves must be content with mediocrity, no matter how impressive their other talents". A similar quote in this vain came from Carnegie's contemporary, Henry Ford who said, "Coming together is a beginning, staying together is progress, and working together is success", that highlights the expectation that workers should adapt to the employer, rather than the other way round.

As in the medieval period workers established communities of common purpose and common interest. In the 16th and 17th century, coffee houses provided ideal environments for like-minded patrons to discuss and debate everything from politics to natural science, "so much so that London coffeehouses became known as 'penny universities', as that was the price of a cup of coffee."[xcix] Luminaries of the time, such as Samuel Pepys, John Dryden, Alexander Pope and Isaac Newton were often seen in polite is sometimes heated discussion over a brew.

"The London Stock Exchange had its beginnings in Jonathan's Coffee House in 1698 where gentlemen met to set stock and

commodity prices. Auctions in salesrooms attached to coffee houses were the beginnings of the great auction houses of Sotheby's and Christies. Lloyd's of London had its origins in Lloyds Coffee House on Lombard Street, run by Edward Lloyd, where merchants, shippers and underwriters of ship insurance met to do business." - Ben Johnson, Historic UK

A century later, during the industrial age labour unions, social clubs and fraternal organisations such as Freemasonry grew increasingly popular. They offered workers, at every level of society, a platform to come together, discuss shared concerns and collaborate on sourcing solutions to various workplace issues. However, they also provided 'members' with the opportunities to develop the soft skills that employers craved. To establish and develop networks, practice organisation and leadership, negotiation and problem solving and communication and teamwork.

Post WW2, economic recovery and growth, technological advancements and globalisation again accelerated the pace of business. Employers now had an increasingly challenging array of requirements for their training programmes. New laws meant new compliance and regulatory training mandates. New sectors interacting with traditional ones led to the need for interdisciplinary education on subjects such as management information systems, organisational development and corporate social responsibility. New technologies required employers to ensure their people could be effective using them, from computers to photocopiers.

These skills were all technical, what an employer needed for their people to ensure they could do their job. But to be truly effective, some employers recognised they needed to shift their learning and development focus from mere productivity to human capital. In 1960's

Japan, Toyota sought to improve its efficiency whilst simultaneously reducing waste. Taiichi Ohno, a managing director at Toyota Motor and Eiji Toyoda an engineer collaborated to develop the Toyota Production System, the core concepts of what would later become known as the 'Toyota Way'. Two elements underpinned it, Just-in-Time "JIT" manufacturing, a method of production influenced by the mass production factories in the USA. And, *Kaizen*, a Japanese term which means, "good change" and "change for the better". For Toyota these principles of self-improvement were adhered by the business and employees alike. "The Toyota style is not to create results by working hard. It is a system that says there is no limit to people's creativity. People don't go to Toyota to 'work'; they go there to 'think'", said Taiichi Ohno.

In America, IBM also recognised that targeting their learning and development at soft skills was critical to ensuring their workforce would operate effectively. In the 1990's, IBM launched an extensive internal program called "Basic Blue", aimed at enhancing essential soft skills, such as communication, teamwork, and problem-solving. Another darling of American industry, General Electric did something similar but their focus was on middle manager training and development. Under the leadership of Jack Welch in the 1980s General Electric created its Leadership Development Centre, which became known as "Crotonville".

Crotonville offered middle managers extensive and rigorous training programs and development opportunities for managers to learn how to be an effective manager. The training was based on the words of Peter Drucker who lived between 1909 and 2005. Drucker is widely considered to be the "Father of Modern Management" and wrote numerous books, such as *The Practice of Management* in 1954, *The Effective Executive* in 1967, and *Management: Tasks, Responsibilities, Practices* in 1973, which formed essential resources for managers and leaders seeking to enhance their management skills and effectiveness.

Drucker was a particular exponent of 'soft skills', (though the terminology was not popularised at the time) in the management process, particularly for middle managers emphasising their role as the driving force for organisational success. He is said to have purported, "The most important thing in communication is to hear what isn't being said", emphasising the role of soft skills for leaders. The investment in manager development by General Electric can be correlated to their impressive performance throughout the 1980s and 1990s. Welch, CEO at this time made his belief clear when he said, "Before you are a leader, success is all about growing yourself. When you become a leader, success is all about growing others".

In response to the pandemic, and lockdown, employers had to instil new ways of working. And, as employees it was necessary to adapt. The unprecedented nature of the challenge lubricated the traditionally slow gears of change within workplaces. Crisis often acts as a catalyst for innovation, particularly within the context of workplaces. This relationship is due to the inherent necessity to adapt, improvise, and overcome challenges that emerge during periods of disruption. For instance, the COVID-19 pandemic forced businesses worldwide to rethink their traditional operating models. This led to a surge in remote working solutions, innovative digital collaboration tools, and new methods of employee engagement. Employers began to value resilience, agility, and digital fluency more than ever before. Moreover, it changed the perception of work as a place to 'be' to work as something we 'do,' fostering a results-oriented culture. Thus, although crises like a global pandemic can be tumultuous and difficult, they also provide fertile ground for innovations that can lead to long-term improvements in the way we work, encouraging businesses to be future-ready and more resilient to upcoming challenges.

Building on this, it's worth considering the role of heuristics, or mental shortcuts, in the workplace. You may not have heard of heuristics, but if you have ever made a decision based on a 'gut feeling' or 'rule-of-thumb' you've practiced heuristics. The Annual Review of Psychology says that "Heuristics are efficient cognitive processes, conscious or unconscious, that ignore part of the information."[c] You could have used heuristics to solve problems or make decisions. Not through detailed, logical analysis, but through the mental shortcuts you've consciously or subconsciously developed through exposure to that environment. They're a valuable tool to that help us quickly come up with good enough, if not always perfect, solutions.

As the pandemic necessitated rapid adaptation, employees found themselves unconsciously leveraging heuristics to efficiently navigate the new remote working environment. Drawing upon past experiences and patterns to swiftly make sense of new software systems, communication platforms, and workflows became a critical survival tool. In essence, the crisis-induced innovation cycle didn't just spur technological advancements but also catalysed shifts in cognitive strategies. Employees' heuristics evolved, guiding on-the-job learning and fostering quick, effective responses to unfamiliar situations. However, while these mental shortcuts expedited decision-making, they also held potential pitfalls.

There is something called the "Horns and Halo" effect. Which along with heuristics is a key cognitive process that shapes our snap judgments. Ever wandered how long you have to make a first impression? Well, research conducted by Princeton psychologists Janine Willis and Alexander Todorov demonstrated that humans often form an initial impression of a stranger's face within just a tenth of a second. Their series of experiments further indicated that prolonging the exposure does not significantly modify these initial impressions. In this way, the "Horns and

Halo" effect can lead us to either overlook negative traits or overemphasise positive ones, skewing our perception of reality and potentially resulting in unfair treatment of individuals.

Why does this matter? Partly, because of unconscious bias, just one of many cognitive prejudices that we use to make decisions or judgments. Unconscious bias, according to Imperial College London, "is a term that describes the associations we hold, outside our conscious awareness and control. Unconscious bias affects everyone"[ci]. This has been corroborated by research conducted by Willis and Todorov highlighted that, "attractive people get better outcomes in practically all walks of life. People with "mature" faces receive more severe judicial outcomes than "baby-faced" people. And having a face that looks competent (as opposed to trustworthy or likeable) may matter a lot in whether a person gets elected to public office"[cii]. As Kahneman highlights, "In about 70% of the races for senator, congressman, and governor, the election winner was the candidate whose face earned a higher rating of confidence"[ciii]. In the run up to the 1960 U.S. presidential elections, both candidates, Nixon and Kennedy took part in debates. In one such debate, simultaneously broadcast over television and radio a very different outcome was reached by those respective audiences in who they rated best. Radio listeners felt Nixon commanded the debate, whilst television viewers were swayed by Kennedy's polished appearance. Kennedy looked the picture of youthful vigour, while a worn-out Nixon, fresh from hospital, struggled visually with a rough shave and noticeable sweat. However, those on radio, absent these visual influences, tuned into the strength of Nixon's arguments.

The thing is this is all unconscious it *affects everyone* – our brains are just conditioned to make these judgement calls. The question is, can they be changed. Irene Blair, PHD, prescribes that, "unconscious biases are not permanent, they are malleable and can be changed by devoting intention, attention, and time to developing new associations"[civ]. This view is not share by everyone, Daniel Kahneman, the Nobel Prize winning phycologist who has spent his life investigating the irrationality of human thought, running "a series of ingenious experiments that revealed twenty or so "cognitive biases" — unconscious errors of reasoning that distort our judgment of the world"[cv]. Reflecting on his career, Kahneman said of unconscious bias, "I know from experience that [overcoming instinctive judgement] is not readily educable"[cvi]. Training for unconscious bias exists, "But while well-intentioned, there's mixed evidence that unconscious-bias training works"[cvii]. Steve Margison, who worked as a Consultant Neuropsychologist before entering the workplace learning field goes further, he says, "all the evidence is unconscious bias training doesn't work. It's pointless because not to be biased, it's how your brain works. We are wired for assumptions, guesses, estimates and generalisations because they're more cognitively efficient, much faster than having to think about things."

Heuristics serve as valuable mental shortcuts for making swift decisions under time constraints, as environments change so do our heuristics, but with the unconscious bias of the "Horns and Halo" effect they may encourage oversimplification and foster prejudices. As Kahneman says, "This is the essence of intuitive heuristics: when faced with a difficult question, we often answer an easier one instead, usually without noticing the substitution"[cviii]. An over-reliance on heuristics can lead to oversimplifications or biases, as these shortcuts might not always capture the complexity of a situation. Therefore, the acceleration of change in the pandemic era underscores the need for workplaces to balance heuristic-based learning with structured training in critical thinking and thorough analysis. As Steve Margison goes on to say, "when the environment forced people to behave in a different way, they did. But as long as you don't reinforce rewards or, you know, punish to some extent the wrong behaviours, things will just keep happening. The same way that people go back to the old ways of behaving, which are more fixed, more rigid, less soup and less agile."

Drawing from this backdrop of rapid adaptation and change, employers turned a keen eye towards learning and development programmes to cultivate resilience, a skill epitomised by 'adaptability.' The pandemic had clearly demonstrated the need for a workforce capable of flexibly responding to unforeseen challenges, pushing adaptability to the forefront. Thus, the call for a workforce equipped to handle unpredictability across all organisational levels became more pronounced, not only as a risk mitigation strategy, but also as a competitive advantage.

Learning management systems "LMS", which had primarily been designed for task-oriented training, found a new purpose. They were repurposed to nurture the in-demand skills necessary for workers to adapt to new ways of working, such as remote collaboration and digital transformation. But the use of LMSs for remote workers was not without its hurdles. Integration challenges were prominent, with many LMS platforms struggling to mesh with key remote tools, leading to disjointed user experiences. UX Issues arose since many LMSs, originally designed for education, didn't match the dynamic needs of remote work, causing user frustrations. Programs suited to a physical work environment just didn't relate to the new world we were inhabiting. Lastly, as companies expanded, certain LMS platforms lagged behind, presenting both scalability issues and unaddressed cybersecurity vulnerabilities associated with remote work. This raises an important question: can these legacy systems effectively deliver not just technical and soft skills but also the requirements of a new world of work?

The need for learning and development programs that balance both technical acuity and soft skills like adaptability becomes paramount. Yet, the methods by which these two types of skills are learned and assimilated can be very different, harking back to the inherent differences between learning and education, and between skills and tradecraft. Although the return on investment for such programs might seem intangible and the engagement levels variable, the need for both skill types remains for employees to be truly effective. Conversely, the education of task-specific knowledge, such as how to use an email platform or follow compliance policies, provides a more tangible and easily measurable return. As Nick Shakleton-Jones says, "Learning is not the product of teaching. Learning is the product of the activity of learners".

The acceleration of two concurrent trends complicates the traditional focus on workplace learning for skills building. Firstly, the volume of human knowledge today is greater than ever before, expanding the potential for innovation but also the need for continual learning. The burgeoning growth in sectors, technologies, and interdisciplinary sciences necessitates that businesses and their employees stay on top of the latest developments and apply them innovatively to their sector. Secondly, the trend of shorter employee tenure challenges the ability of employers to recoup the costs of learning and development training, while ensuring business-critical knowledge is efficiently transferred within employers.

Knowledge

There's a folktale I love, from the Akan people of modern-day Ghana. The story is of Anasi (which translates as "spider"), the god of stories, knowledge and trickery. In one fable, Anansi wanted to gather all the world's wisdom in a pot for safekeeping. After collecting wisdom from across the globe, he took the pot to a tall, thorny tree for hiding. His son, Ntikuma, followed him, witnessing Anansi struggling to climb the tree with the large pot tied in front. Ntikuma suggested tying the pot behind him, which annoyed Anansi so much that the pot fell and shattered, spilling all his collected wisdom. A sudden storm washed the wisdom into a nearby stream, from where it spread to the entire world. Anansi's plan to hoard wisdom failed, instead, it ended up being shared with everyone.

Employers have long sought to collect and safeguard their knowledge, the combination of data, information, and skills that employees acquire through experience or education, and store it safely. As employees have left, that knowledge has leaked or had been forgotten as the employee had not shared it before departing. The great resignation of 2021, in the wake of the pandemic could have been the storm that Anasi experienced. Turning the leak of employer knowledge into a flood. However, most employers had infrastructure in place. A little more robust than that of Anasi, the spider god.

Knowledge Management Systems (KMS) had first developed in the 1990s, in conjunction with the concept of the 'Learning Organisation' popularised by the American systems scientist and MIT Lecturer, Peter Senge. In his book, 'The Fifth Discipline', Senge emphasised the importance of organisational learning and knowledge sharing to both contend with the growing pool of human knowledge and the realisation, that harnessing it would offer an employer a competitive advantage.

Whilst employers have developed solutions for securing knowledge, imparting it upon new employees remains a challenge. Firstly, the diverse nature of the workforce, with varying backgrounds, experiences, and learning styles (as we've explored), means a one-size-fits-all approach to knowledge sharing is seldom effective. Employers must seek solutions that provide a more personalised, flexible learning experience. The issue here is that this can be both time-consuming and costly.

Secondly, the combination of globalisation and digitalisation has led to an explosion of knowledge, relevant to employers and employees alike. To exemplify the extraordinary exponential growth of human knowledge here are a few stats:

- *In 1900, 10,000 scientific articles were being published annually, by the year 2000 the number was 1 million, an increase of 9900%.*

- *In 1985, there were roughly 630,000 patent applications filed globally, while in 2018, this number had risen to over 3.3 million applications*

- *In 2013, Google estimated that the digital universe contained approximately 5 zettabytes of data (1 zettabyte equals 1 trillion gigabytes, 1 gigabyte is about 240 songs on an MP3 player). By 2020, the digital universe had grown to 40 zettabytes*

New technologies and constant seeking of a competitive advantage results in continuous learning, adaption and experimentation, all of which results in additional knowledge. For employers, balancing the urgency of meeting immediate business needs with the time required for meaningful knowledge sharing can be tricky. For example, in a law firm, you might have a partner who has recently worked on data security in artificial intelligence. Whilst there will be a written account that their colleagues could read to learn from, nothing is quite as valuable as talking to that individual. But if that individual now has a mountain of work coming in from paying clients what they don't have is time. Compounding that challenge is if that individual works from home, so they can't even be ambushed by a junior colleague desperate to learn from them as they navigate the office.

Thirdly, much of the knowledge within an organisation is tacit—it resides in people's minds and is often difficult to articulate and codify. This poses a challenge for knowledge transfer, particularly when experienced employees leave or in large organisations operating remotely. The water cooler moments have gone, instead, employees must reach out to colleagues that they may never have met in person. The report, *The Modern Workplace Demands a New Approach to Knowledge Management,* says, "A prevalent problem in organizations today is that employees simply cannot know everyone in the organization: 28% of respondents say their organization is too large to know who might have answers, and 25% say they often don't know who to contact when a problem arises."[cix]

In recent years we've seen the average employee tenure fall drastically. The climax of employee voluntary turnover came in the wake of the Coronavirus pandemic with 'The Great Resignation'. According to the US Bureau of Labor, The Great Resignation saw a record-breaking 4.4 million people voluntarily quit their jobs.

But what caused this mass exodus of human capital? The Harvard Business Review chalks the huge surge in Americans (the study focussed on the USA, but the effects of the Great Resignation were global) leaving their jobs up to five factors; retirement, relocation, reconsideration, reshuffling, and reluctance. Retirement in this case is not as self-explanatory as it once was. Many chose retirement, not because of age but because of lifestyle changes. The pandemic prompted, "millions to reassess their relationship to their jobs"[cx]. The break from traditional workspaces offered a chance for introspection, leading many to retire early, seeking less stressful, more fulfilling lives or even commoditise hobbies that they'd fostered with their increased time at home. Retirement therefore not from work, but from the workplace.

Relocation again wasn't from one workplace to another as it had been prior to the pandemic, but from a physical location to a virtual one. The acceptance and possibility of remote work gave people the opportunity to choose how and where to work. I think of remote working as the forbidden fruit of workplaces. Once tried, very few want to go back, as Unispace's, *The Reluctance Report* highlighted, "the majority of workers polled across Europe (64%) are worried about a return to the workplace".

The remaining three factors also present a compelling case for employers to act. Reconsideration is similar to the above, but I would argue is driven primarily by individuals assessing their mental health and work-life balance. COVID-19 again played a pivotal role, as people witnessed family members passing away and were unable to provide support due to lockdowns or travel restrictions. Burnout, a term frequently tossed around in the business realm, often remains unnoticed by employees until it's too late. The pandemic made burnout painfully apparent, as leaders, first-responders, and caregivers were stretched to their limits without ample rest or recuperation time. With women constituting the majority of caregiving roles, it wasn't surprising that, in 2021, one in three women considered leaving their professions, switching jobs, or reducing their weekly hours.

In industries such as finance and consulting, the pressure to work harder and longer intensified during the pandemic and beyond, given the widespread uncertainty. Many employees in these fields struggled with the long hours and lack of in-person benefits such as mentorship and social interaction with clients and colleagues. For many, the mental, physical, and emotional toll was no longer worth it.

Reshuffling refers to the desire for change, as individuals become dissatisfied with their current company or industry and seek alternative opportunities. In 2022, Bharata Ramamurti of the US National Economic Council coined "the Great Upgrade" to describe individuals quitting low-wage industries in large numbers. The trend extended beyond the pandemic-stricken food and leisure/hospitality sectors, affecting professional and business services too. The widespread employment gaps in numerous industries suggest that people weren't just looking for new companies, but entirely different sectors. The problem with L&D lies within this reshuffling phenomenon. If employees aren't satisfied with their current work and don't feel they can grow, learn, or nurture new skills, they're willing to switch companies or industries to achieve their desired goals. This willingness to accept a pay cut and lower position in pursuit of passion should be a wake-up call for companies to invest more in employee retention and development.

Finally, we need to look at reluctance. In a corporate setting reluctance refers to staff hesitance to fully commit to tasks or organisational changes. Various triggers exist—from workload hikes and poor management to lack of motivation or fear of the unfamiliar. Reluctance is likely to result in lower productivity or less enthusiasm, and if unchecked, could hamper the company's success. A new term entered our corporate lexicon, "quiet quitting". Quiet quitting refers to those "not engaged at work -- people who do the minimum required and are psychologically detached from their job"[cxi]. And, quiet quitting is on the rise. In the US, according to research by Gallup in 2022, "The ratio of engaged to actively disengaged employees is now 1.8 to 1, the lowest in almost a decade".

Over the years, this extraordinary decline in employee tenure and engagement has been driven by a range of factors, such as an increasingly accessible job market, technological advancements making it easier to work remotely and changing attitudes and expectations of what work is and means for employees. As we've seen, the pandemic was for many the final straw.

The repercussion of this increased transitionary workforce and ever-growing pot of knowledge is a challenge for employers. Essentially, there is more they need to impart and all in a shorter amount of time. To ensure their people can execute business strategy as quickly and efficiently as possible. Employers across the globe now have to consider how they can leverage learning and development initiatives to both secure and preserve vast repositories of information gleaned from the workforce and to then effectively regurgitate. As part of their succession planning to new employees who require it to perform their roles proficiently.

With remote working, the challenge has clearly grown. Employers must now transmit knowledge and nurse technical and soft skills, faster and with fewer touch points than ever before.

What an employer needs from learning and development has spurred investment and a flurry of new approaches and programmes in their people's development. But, a significant challenge persists, stemming from the intangible nature of outcomes and the complexity of the initiatives and variety of peoples involved. That learning and development continues to struggle to measure return on investment. "The most elusive element in L&D is often the quantification of its impact", says Professor Dr. John Sullivan, an American based author and industry commentator.

As we have seen from what an employer needs of learning and development today, programmes are necessarily multi-faceted and encompass a wide range of approaches such as eLearning, workshops, conferences and social interaction. This mish mash of activities makes it difficult to isolate specific contributions to success. Furthermore, the effects when they are realised often taken place over a prolonged period of time as employees gradually acquire and apply the knowledge and skills that the business needs. The indeterminable period of real learning return-on-investment is a total juxtaposition to the quarterly reporting that most companies adhere to.

This is not unique to L&D, other verticals within businesses such as marketing, corporate social responsibility and wellness programs also face similar challenges when attesting to value versus spend. As Guy Stephens, head of microlearning at IBM recounted, this dilemma "Reminds me of when people asked back in the early days of social media: *What is the ROI of social media?* And because people didn't know how to answer it, because it hadn't been worked out adequately yet, they answered – *what is the ROI of not doing it!?*".

But this puts L&D, and these sectors at risk when budgets are cut, or further investment allocated. Employers clearly know that there is value in L&D and know that their employees are asking for it, so it must be of some worth. The biggest problem is that companies think about two things above just about everything else: How do we measure something to see how valuable it is, and what the bottom line is: basically, is this *thing* costing us money or making us money?

Workplace Learning and Compliance

C ompliance has offered employers an opportunity to tangibly deliver learning and development training with measurable results – results that sometimes had less to do with development and more to do with protection. "In order to improve return on investment, historically L&D is focused on the risk management side of things. Corporate training is risk mitigation," says Dr Ashwin Mehta, Head of Global Learning Technologies at Bayer. "Let's say we send out a bit of knowledge to 1,000 and 900 of them do it. What does that tell us? Not much; it's a lot like measuring seat time in a classroom. They attended, they filled the seats, but we can't tell how much people have learned. "In the modern world, we have increasing capability to gather granular data but only if the profession itself has digital literacy to capitalise on data. What data do we need to collect? We have to get to the point where we are using data effectively."

In April 2010, off the United States coast in the Gulf of Mexico an environmental catastrophe unfolded. The largest marine oil spill in history happened at the BP run, Deepwater Horizon resulting in deaths and huge environmental damage resulting in $65bn in fines. In the aftermath, BP identified a pressing need to overhaul its safety and compliance culture. To address this issue, BP instituted a comprehensive learning and development program, integrating safety leadership and compliance training across the entire organisation. This initiative included compulsory e-learning courses, interactive workshops, and immersive simulation experiences, all aimed at cultivating a deep understanding of the significance of compliance and the ramifications of non-compliance among employees. Bob Dudley, BP's former CEO, spoke years later about the company's efforts to learn from the incident, "We have learned from those events and are applying the lessons internally and externally. Safety is our first priority".

Learning and development provided BP with an opportunity to demonstrate they were taking action. Yes, to train up their people (though the cause of the catastrophe related to poor quality cement on the well head), but also to hold them to account. Murray Auchincloss, BP's Chief Financial Officer says, "BP's L&D initiatives have driven the development of a stronger, more mature safety culture. Our focus is on ensuring everyone understands their role in creating a safe and compliant work environment". Is this protection for employees, or for the employer? By ensuring that employees were trained, they had little excuse for when things went wrong. For example, in 2011, BP fired Robert Kaluza, a well site leader on the Deepwater Horizon rig, citing *'failure to provide responsible supervision of contractors'* and *'failure to identify risk related to the Macondo well'*. Another well site leader, Donald Vidrine, was initially demoted but later retired in 2012. Both Kaluza and Vidrine were also charged with manslaughter (later reduced to misdemeanour Clean Water Act violations), to which they pleaded not guilty and were eventually acquitted. Compliance training therefore provides employers with a crucial safeguard, which can shield the employer from potential litigation, and the associated financial and reputational risk. By ensuring that Learning and Development is providing comprehensive compliance training, ensuring that employees are aware of applicable laws, regulations and policies the likelihood of a violation that could trigger legal action is reduced. But, if a breach does occur, demonstrating that the employer has made concerted efforts to educate its workforce significantly mitigates the employer's liability.

Bob Dudely, and the executive team at BP knew that being seen to take action in the wake of Deepwater Horizion was critical: critical to shareholders. For a relatively modest investment, learning and development could be used as the blunt weapon to repair BP's reputation, demonstrate industry leadership, placate corporate social responsibility concerns and rebuild trust with stakeholders, including investors, regulators customers and the public by appearing transparent. Dudley emphasised this by advocating the importance of transparently sharing learnings from the disaster, by saying, "It's essential that we share these lessons across the industry so we can help prevent such an incident happening again".

BP is not alone, Siemens, a global technology and engineering megalith was facing numerous allegations of corruption and bribery in the early 2000s which led to Siemens paying approximately $1.6bn in fines to U.S. and German authorities. In response, the company implemented the 'Siemens Integrity Initiative', which focusses on compliance training for employees. These efforts have paid off, as Siemens has managed to avoid major fines or allegations of corruption since the launch of the Integrity Initiative. The success of the program has contributed to Siemens regaining its reputation as a responsible and ethical business, demonstrating the effectiveness of robust compliance measures in mitigating the risks associated with corporate misconduct.

Not every L&D initiative in compliance training follows an enormous fine, but the potential cost lends weight to investment. But, there is another aspect of what employers want from learning and development that adheres to compliance training. That is its compulsory nature. Compliance training is compulsory, take IMB for example, with its

Business Conduct Guidelines which every employee has to complete every year, and are publicly available. Employees must accept education in compliance, therefore universal engagement is guaranteed.

In Summary

I think it's pretty clear that the traditional paradigms of workplace learning have been disrupted. The incessant growth of human knowledge and technologies continues to reshape the landscape of skills and competencies employers seek from their workforce. Simultaneously, the erosion of lengthy employee tenure and the rise of remote work poses new challenges for knowledge management, succession planning and sharing. Like a sandbar, as soon as it's mapped it's changed.

Workplace learning has moved well beyond the confines of imparting technical expertise; it's now about fostering a culture of perpetual learning that blends technical acuity with softer skills like adaptability, emotional intelligence and resilience. The challenge, however, lies in creating a learning ecosystem that is flexible enough to accommodate this broad spectrum of skills, targeted enough to provide relevant learning opportunities and robust enough to provide measurable returns.

Traditional education-oriented systems often struggle with this task, as they're primarily designed to produce quantifiable outcomes. Compliance training provides a clear case in point. As an essential aspect of workplace learning, compliance training presents easily trackable

ROI—employees either complete the required training and adhere to the rules, or they don't. It's straightforward, black and white.

Learning, however, is a more nebulous concept. It involves not only the acquisition of knowledge but also its application in novel contexts. It's a lifelong process of growth and adaptation that doesn't fit neatly into the confines of our current educational systems. In other words, teaching a skill is not the same as learning it. As John Holt writes, "Learning is not the product of teaching. Learning is the product of the activity of learners."

So, what can employers do to address their learning needs more effectively in this complex, ever-evolving context?

Firstly, there needs to be a shift from a purely education-based approach to a learning-centred one that accommodates both the technical and soft skills necessary for the modern workforce. This could involve the integration of innovative learning methodologies, like experiential learning or gamification, that engage employees in active learning.

Secondly, it's crucial for employers to understand and appreciate the role of heuristics, the mental shortcuts that workers employ in everyday decision-making. By recognizing the dual-edged nature of heuristics—both as facilitators of efficient decision-making and potential sources of bias—employers can tailor training programs to foster more effective heuristics and mitigate the less desirable ones.

Thirdly, given the shorter tenure of employees, employers need to reconsider their strategies for knowledge transfer and retention. This could involve creating robust succession plans, fostering a culture of knowledge sharing, and leveraging technology to create knowledge repositories.

Lastly, in an era where knowledge is vast and continually evolving, it's incumbent upon employers to foster a culture of lifelong learning. Employers need to empower their employees to take charge of their learning journey, encouraging them to keep abreast of the latest developments in their fields and apply this newfound knowledge innovatively within their roles. All within the context of the time, whether this is classroom-based instruction if everyone is in the office or a shift to the "cell phone, where learning takes place in the juncture between work, leisure and home life" explain Guy Stephens.

In summary, workplace learning is at a crossroads. By embracing a learning-centred approach, acknowledging the role of heuristics, reconsidering knowledge management strategies, and fostering a culture of lifelong learning, employers can better align their workplace learning initiatives with their needs in this digital age. The task is complex, but the rewards are manifold—a more adaptable, innovative, and resilient workforce ready to tackle whatever the future may bring.

But there are two parties in this dance – now let's look into the needs of the other one: employees.

iii. What do Employees Want from L&D?

"94% of employees say that they would stay at a company longer if it invested in their learning and development." – LinkedIn's 2021 Workplace Learning Report

Employees are not a homogenous group; they of course never have been. Each person brings their own set of experiences, backgrounds, perspectives, skills and learning approaches to the table. Whilst diversity is now espoused by employers, with individuality on the face of it encouraged, this wasn't always the case. Throughout history, employers have squashed individuality, to various extents, in exchange for streamlining operations and increasing productivity. Gary Hamel, a Visiting Professor of Strategy and Entrepreneurship at London Business School affirms this in his book, *The Future of Management*, highlights that, "In the past, organisations sought efficiency and productivity by imposing a one-size-fits-all approach". He goes on to say that "to management and work, individuality was seen as a threat to order and predictability"[cxii]. This has included establishing uniforms and dress-codes, discouraging independent thought and relying on strict hierarchies. Whilst there are plenty of case studies I could reference, the truth is you probably have direct experiences of this yourself.

Over the years, the workplace has grown to be more accepting of individual differences. There is little surprise that this shift coincided with the developments of social technology. As social media platforms surged in popularity, a new era dawned where employees began to recognise

120

and celebrate their individuality with greater self-determination. Over time, technological advancements, globalisation, and progressive social norms converged to create workplaces that value diversity and inclusion. This environment has not only empowered individuals to seamlessly extend their authenticity - "to be their true selves" - from their personal lives into their professional sphere but has also instilled a desire to express their distinct backgrounds, perspectives, and identities at work. Beyond just personal expression, employees were now actively holding their employers to account, ensuring that organisational values align with their own.

Let's explore that last sentence a little – as the difference between what companies say and what they do, commonly referred to as 'stated versus actual values' is a critical subject. Stated values are the principles that companies proudly present in their mission statements and on their websites. These are the ideals they strive to uphold, at least on paper. Actual values, on the other hand, are the true principles in action, seen in the day-to-day decisions and behaviours of the company.

Now, when there's a considerable gap between stated and actual values, it becomes a source of unease among employees. Imagine a company that pledges 'transparency' but keeps its decision-making process cloaked in secrecy. Or a firm that claims to prioritise 'employee welfare' but disregards the importance of work-life balance. Such inconsistencies can raise eyebrows and lead to a wave of scepticism among the workforce.

The fallout? A growing sense of mistrust and a spike in cynicism, eroding the very fabric of the organisational culture. In today's evolving workplace, it's paramount for companies to align their words with their actions. This consistency is the cornerstone of authenticity, trust, and ultimately, employee engagement. To ensure that employees feel that they belong, not a word used enough. Indeed, when the gap between stated and actual values becomes too noticeable, it can lead to a real crisis of confidence. Historically, companies might have gotten away with this discrepancy to some extent. After all, information wasn't as readily accessible, and employees often didn't have the platforms to voice their concerns.

However, with the digital age, the balance of power has shifted. Employees now have access to vast amounts of information and, importantly, the means to share their experiences broadly. We've seen a significant rise in employee activism. No longer are staff members silent bystanders; instead, they're active participants, unafraid to hold their employers accountable for perceived injustices or inconsistencies.

The consequences of this shift can be far-reaching. For a start, a company can face reputational damage, a public backlash even. No organisation wants to trend on social media for all the wrong reasons. Moreover, internal morale can take a hit, leading to decreased productivity, increased turnover, and difficulties in attracting top talent. When trust is lost, rebuilding it is no small feat and can drain significant time, energy, and resources.

Employee activism is not an entirely new phenomenon, the subjugated of every age have fought injustice with the means at their disposal. What we have come to recognise today as employee activism probably developed in the industrial age, in the same workers clubs and labour unions that we recognised earlier in this book as breeding and practice grounds for social skills. The first recorded worker organised uprising was in Lyon, France, in 1831, and called the Canut Revolts. This harbinger of employee activism started decades of civil unrest characterised by strikes and worker militancy. But France was not alone, across Western nations workers campaigned for fairer wages, safer working conditions and reasonable working hours.

Successive social campaigns, particularly those for universal suffrage, civil rights and LGBTQ+ resulted in legislation entrenching the right of the individual in many countries. These, in turn were further buoyed with the advent of the digital age. As the internet and social media played a pivotal role in amplifying voices of minorities that had typically been drowned out in the past. Even before the pandemic, we saw things like the 2018 Google walkouts that were staged to demand sweeping changes to the company, including curbing forced arbitration, stopping pay inequality between men and women, the promotion of a Chief of Diversity, and a complete overhaul to the process of reporting sexual misconduct and harassment. According to news reports, a staggering 20,000 people, about 20% of the company's total number of employees, participated in the protests. In 2019, Microsoft employees rallied against their company signing a contract for $480 million to provide the U.S. Army with headsets for augmented reality training. Employees published a petition on Twitter demanding the company not get involved as *war profiteers*. Today, numerous networks and platforms exist that empower employees to raise grievances, establish communities, mobilise activity and promote and publicise their goals.

So why does this matter for workplace learning? Well, in the past workforce training was unidirectional. Employers would tell employees what they wanted them to learn. To perform better, be compliant etc. and that was that. If the employee didn't like it, they could leave. As we've recognised in previous chapters on the history of workplace learning and the needs of employers, people metamorphosed from craftspeople protected by their inherent knowledge to cogs and gears within the ever-expanding machinery of commerce. The role of workplace learning was to fashion that *gear,* and to ensure any replacement parts could be utilised immediately.

Today, employee activism has upset this black and white view by adding colour. Employee activism has realigned traditional hierarchies as people have called to be recognised as individuals – with their own values and needs – not as uniform gears. Channels for communication are now far more omnidirectional, with employees able to champion issues that are important to them and make demands of their employers to help them grow in their careers.

To see this in practice I'd like to introduce two characters; Beatrice and Kalm. Their paths had crossed at university, where they studied marketing together. Now, as fresh graduates with nearly identical resume's and degrees and grade-point averages, they found themselves competing in the challenging job market. Despite their many similarities, they were about to discover that their differing approaches to learning would significantly impact their professional journeys.

Fate intervened on one particular day when both Beatrice and Kalm found themselves interviewing at different, yet prestigious, marketing firms. As if guided by an unseen hand, their interviews unfolded in parallel, with each being asked the same questions. The interviewers at Beatrice's firm excitedly spoke about the revolutionary use of Artificial Intelligence (AI) and Machine Learning (ML) in their digital marketing campaigns. They asked Beatrice about her proficiency with these technologies, eager to determine if she would be a valuable addition to their innovative team. Across town, Kalm was also getting similar questions as his firm espoused the benefits of AI and ML revolutionising the way that they create campaigns, target customer segments, find trends and patterns in Big Data that would have taken their human equivalents weeks or months to figure out and are able to make recommendations on which direction to take campaigns.

This was cutting edge stuff, and far more advanced than the subject matter of their degree at university, which clearly lagged behind what was going on in the corporate world by some margin. Both Beatrice and Kalm were keenly aware that admitting their lack of expertise might ruin their chances of securing a job. So, driven by ambition and necessity, they both feigned understanding and enthusiasm. As luck would have it, their performances were convincing enough to land them second interviews and eventually job offers at their respective firms.

Once they secured their positions, Beatrice and Kalm's paths diverged. Fuelled by a need to make good on her perceived understanding of AI and ML, Beatrice chose to tackle her knowledge gap head-on. She signed up to a MOOC on digital marketing, downloaded software demos, watched hours of YouTube video explainers and prepared flashcards to sound knowledgeable about the subject. Beatrice was also a natural networker, she attended numerous events and built up a community of professionals who she felt comfortable asking for advice and explanations. Through hard work, social interactions and determination, she aimed to become the expert she had claimed to be.

Kalm, on the other hand, chose a different approach. He believed he could learn what was needed of him on the job. In his mind, he would simply wing it, pick up the necessary skills as he went along, and no one would be any the wiser.

Then the pandemic hit. The office was closed and both Beatrice and Kalm were required to work from home. Kalm soon found himself lost and confused when given his first assignment, which involved using the company's customised AI software. He quickly realised that winging it wouldn't work in this situation. If he were in the office, a simple nudge and whisper to a colleague could have solved his problem. But the transactional nature of working from home, instant messaging and publicly visible message boards made him anxious to ask for help. Fearful of being exposed Kalm chose instead to isolate himself from his peers. As the software was customised to his company, his only option was to comb through countless links and documents in the company's knowledge management system, desperately hoping to find a manual or guide that could save him from admitting his initial deception.

Beatrice's story, in contrast, took a more positive turn. Her relentless preparation and dedication to learning paid off as she quickly became an invaluable team member at her firm. Her network, that she continued to nurture throughout lockdown proved to be invaluable, ensuring she was abreast of the latest trend, development and approach. What's more she was happy to present what she had learnt on the latest technological advance and trend to other members of the team, inadvertently taking on a leadership role with the group. Her colleagues were impressed by her knowledge and sought her out for more projects and advice. As Beatrice continued to excel in her job, her employer recognised the importance of investing in her development. They offered her opportunities for further training and mentorship, to join the 'High-Performer/Future-Leader Program', a well-funded learning and development initiative, and, to take on more responsibilities which allowed her to practice her new found skillsets and expertise. Beatrice embraced these opportunities, believing that continuous learning was not only essential to remaining relevant and competitive in the marketing industry but also to give her confidence to take on more challenges such as running a team of her own.

Kalm's journey, though rockier than Beatrice's, was not without hope. As he struggled with learning about the systems his firm used and interacting socially with colleagues, he found that he had a passion for Big Data and Kalm became fascinated by how data could be used more effectively to influence their marketing approach. He was particularly interested, practically obsessively, in identifying trends that improved the success of their marketing conversions to particular groups and demographics. Kalm began to seek out learning resources as Beatrice had done, favouring books over conversations, and driven by interest he created a tool that aggregated company information and provided recommendations. In most of Kalm's one-to-one meetings with his manager he was monosyllabic, apparently disinterested in work. But, on hearing about Kalm's passion, his manager asked him to share what he had learnt. Kalm lit up at the opportunity and excitedly presented his solution to his manager, who was dumbstruck, was this really the same Kalm from one week ago? Kalm's passion project had resulted in a creative and useful solution for his employer that was immediately implemented, and Kalm was moved to another team, where he prospered.

This parable isn't morally perfect but perhaps more accurate of real-life then we'd like to admit. Both Kalm and Beatrice felt the need to *fib* to their prospective employers about their subject understanding. Perhaps they were nervous and keen to impress, perhaps this was interview seventeen with twelve different companies and they were desperate. I'm not condoning this embellishment – but I think it's not unusual, apparently more prevalent amongst men than women, and can you honestly say you've never done it? I certainly have. Coming out of university or school with what you consider to be a solid grasp of your chosen subject, only to have that impression dashed to pieces like an ice-cube in a blender, in your first contact with an employer practicing in the space.

If we explore the aspirations of employees like Kalm and Beatrice sheds light on what they seek from their employer's learning and development program. Initially, they desire a bridge between their formal education and the practical demands of their work, easing the transition and enhancing their work readiness. Secondly, a recognition of individuality is crucial, as it tailors the learning experience to their unique capabilities and learning curves, making the process more engaging and effective. Furthermore, they anticipate the cultivation of soft skills through a variety of methods, enriching their interpersonal interactions and problem-solving abilities. Lastly, a flexible and supportive learning environment is key, providing a conducive atmosphere for continuous growth, exploration, and the application of newly acquired skills in real-world scenarios.

Let's look at these in more detail.

To bridge the gap between formal education and work

The experience of Beatrice and Kalm resonates with many individuals, myself included, as they navigate the transition from formal education to the workplace. As Oscar Wilde once wittily remarked, "Education is an admirable thing, but it is well to remember from time to time that nothing that is worth knowing can be taught"[cxiii]. Although intended as a humorous quip, this sentiment rings true for Beatrice and Kalm, who, despite their impressive academic achievements, found themselves lacking the practical knowledge and skills required in their professional lives.

As we examine the experiences of Beatrice and Kalm, we uncover several key factors that contribute to the gap between formal education and workplace readiness. The outdated curriculums in academic institutions often lags behind industry advancements, leaving graduates ill-prepared for their professional endeavours. Additionally, the traditional emphasis on theoretical knowledge over practical experience in educational settings does little to develop hands-on skills necessary for success. Furthermore, the lack of flexibility in the learning environment may hinder students' ability to adapt to the dynamic demands of modern workplaces. It is also worth noting that the limited connections between academia and industry can deprive students of valuable real-world experiences and practical insights. Lastly, the insufficient focus on soft skill development within formal education means that essential skills such as communication, critical thinking, and teamwork are often overlooked.

To address these shortcomings, a symbiotic relationship between academia and industry is essential, with one informing and supporting the other. In this way, the understanding of the *'why'* behind human interactions in the workplace, particularly in relation to motivation, can be significantly enhanced. This especially rings true for individuals who garner workplace experience before pursuing higher education. Employees like Beatrice and Kalm can draw connections between the theoretical frameworks they encounter academically and their practical on-the-ground knowledge. This blend of experiences ultimately leads to richer learning, more effective leadership, and better support systems. This also underscores the importance of initiatives such as internships and co-ops, which are sadly becoming rarer and rarer, offering the much-needed taste of real-world scenarios before a full plunge into the workplace. So, it's not about pitting academia against industry, but harmonising them for a more comprehensive and industry-relevant educational approach.

To recognise individuality

I ndividuality has been a theme throughout this and the previous chapter. Indeed, we recognised the different type of learners right at the beginning of this book. It's important that employers recognise in action, that employees are not a homogenous group. Beatrice and Kalm are just two examples, who received similar interviews and secured similar outcomes -both at similar stages of their lives.

But what if Beatrice and Kalm had another new-joiner in their intake. Let's call them Sophia. Our graduates are ripe with potential, like a blank slate – they are enthusiastic, adaptable, but lack professional experience. On the flip side, Sophia has been working in this sector for 25 years. They bring a wealth of industry and professional experience.

So that's set the scene, let me introduce two terms we are yet to cover in this book; 'pedagogy' and 'andragogy'. You may well have come across these terms before, **pedagogy**, is the traditional form of teaching, involving a one-directional flow of knowledge from teacher to student – like master to apprentice. In contrast, **andragogy**, is a term popularised by adult educator Malcolm Knowles, and is a more learner-centric approach that values the experiences and self-directedness of the learner. "Adults need to know why they need to learn something before undertaking to learn it", explains Knowles. Andragogy suggests that adults are autonomous and intrinsically motivated learners, who draw upon their wealth of experience as they learn.

In a workplace setting, these two philosophies can have dramatically different implications. Pedagogical approaches may translate into structured training sessions or workshops where information is disseminated by a trainer. On the other hand, an andragogical approach might be reflected in more collaborative exercises such as group problem-solving tasks or experiential learning initiatives.

Both Kalm and Beatrice experienced pedagogical learning from their years in university - receiving knowledge in a structured manner. For them, a similar approach in the workplace might be beneficial, initially. Structured training sessions, clear guidance, and constructive feedback can help transition them from academic theory to industry practice.

On the flip side, Sophia's learning style aligns more with andragogy, valuing self-direction and application of prior knowledge. She's likely to appreciate collaborative projects and problem-solving exercises, where she can share her insights from her own experience and learn from the experiences of others.

Indeed, the training needs of Kalm, Beatrice and Sophia are different. Their unique stages in life - one at the beginning of their careers, and the other a seasoned professional - necessitate different learning approaches. Therefore, it's crucial for workplaces to adopt a flexible training strategy, balancing structured, pedagogical training for less experienced staff with more collaborative, andragogical approaches for those with a wealth of experience. Such a strategy could lead to more effective training, ensuring that all employees, regardless of their life stage, are equipped to excel.

In our earlier story, we can see how both Kalm and Beatrice learned to their strengths. Once realising the value of knowledge assimilation, they approached it in their own way. Beatrice thrives in social interactions and relishes developing networks, using them to learn what she needs. Kalm's temperament is quite the opposite, he's perceived as being more introverted as he goes about learning in a different way.

Neither employee is inherently more intelligent or valuable than the other, but it could be argued that Beatrice fits the traditional mould of what an employer might expect from their team members. Historically, extroverts have often been seen as more successful due to their ease in engaging with others. A study by the "University of Toronto Scarborough has found that extroverts do have an edge that boosts their chances of success"[cxiv]. This perception may arise from extroverts' tendencies to be outgoing and excel in social situations, as well as their confidence in assuming leadership roles and management responsibilities—qualities frequently linked with success in the business world. "If you're motivated to achieve a goal at work, if you're feeling positive, and if you're good at dealing with people, you're probably going to perform better on the job," says Michael Wilmot, the academic who led the study. "These advantages appear to have a cumulative effect over the span of one's career"[cxv].

This can have implications for learning and development, particularly when it comes to targeting education programs for perceived "talent" or "future leaders." If businesses view public speaking and networking as attributes of a successful leader, they might unintentionally favour extroverts over introverts, perpetuating a self-fulfilling prophecy in which the next generation of leaders possess these qualities, solidifying them as necessary attributes for such programs.

Just like Kalm, not every employee is extroverted—similarly, the same argument can be made for all aspects of diversity present in the workplace. Any learning and development program that focuses on a specific "type" of employee risks alienating and failing to nurture diverse talents like Kalm. If not for his manager, would anyone in the company have realised the hidden gem they had in Kalm? Or would historical biases continue to hinder diversity in the workforce? Ultimately, employees are seeking learning and development opportunities that don't pigeonhole them into a particular category but instead acknowledge and celebrate their individuality.

The wider acceptance and encouragement of individuality across an increasingly connected society ensures that employers have to recognise and support diversity in their organisations. This is particularly relevant when it comes to leadership development programs, a shift that is not only important for fairness but also to seize commercial opportunities. As Satya Nadella, CEO of Microsoft, once said, "Our industry does not respect tradition – it only respects innovation." The key players, revenue generators, and business leaders of today differ vastly from those of a decade or a century ago, and they will continue to evolve in the coming years.

To cultivate soft skills in a myriad of ways

The skills, qualities, attitudes that have traditionally been valued by employers are likely to evolve as well. Consequently, fostering diversity is not a 'nice-to-have' exercise but instead a key ingredient for competitive advantage. We can think of this as equitable learning, which underscores the importance of providing every individual, like Sarah, Kalm and Beatrice with the necessary tools and opportunities to achieve their potential, taking into consideration the diverse ways in which people process information. Central to this is recognising neurodiversity, the understanding that variations in the human brain regarding sociability, learning, attention, mood, and other functions are natural and should be respected. Neurodiverse individuals, such as those with autism, ADHD, dyslexia, and other neurological differences, bring unique strengths and perspectives. By creating learning environments that are flexible and adaptable to diverse neurocognitive needs, we not only support the well-being and success of neurodiverse individuals but also foster richer, more inclusive communities that benefit from a breadth of thought and experience. For Kalm, perhaps his value could have been realised and developed sooner with a program that recognised him for all that he was. At the very least, this would have created a more inclusive environment. Where employees irrespective of their differences are more likely to feel valued.

Whilst Beatrice was recognised for fitting the mould of a successful employee early on in her career, Kalm's value took longer to bring to light. Both Beatrice and Kalm, one through the learning and development program and the other through the personal interjection of their manager (*I'm a big fan of middle management – and we will touch more on this workplace layer later in the book*) resulted in significant contributions for their respective employers. By recognising individuality and cultivating a culture of continuous learning and personal growth across the diversity of their workplace, companies can nurture talent who bring a wealth of unique experiences, ideas, and attributes to the table.

The risk if they don't is stark. In 2001, a plan long orchestrated by Al Qaeda leader, Osama bin Laden reached its appalling finale. In the aftermath of 9/11, a commission was established to examine how the Central Intelligence Agency could have missed this threat. As Matthew Syed highlights, "A startlingly high proportion of staff at the CIA had grown up in middle class families, endured little financial hardship, or the signs that might act as precursors to radicalisation, or any of a multitude of other experiences that might have added formative insights to the intelligence process". What Matthew is describing is *perspective blindness*, a form of bias where routine thinking patterns become so ingrained that they go unnoticed. As then CIA director, John Brennan concluded after an internal review, "The study group took a hard look at our agency and reached an unequivocal conclusion: CIA simply must do more to develop the diverse and inclusive leadership environment that our values require and that our mission demands"[cxvi].

This example is obviously extreme, but it serves to highlight the value of encouraging and supporting diversity across all levels. By doing so, entities can break longstanding biases, like favouring extroverts over introverts, and simultaneously nurture each employee's potential, reminiscent of Kalm's journey. The outcome? An institution that's not only more dynamic and resilient but also markedly successful.

The lack of soft skill training was registered earlier in this chapter when we were exploring the shortcomings of further education to prepare students for the workplace. But what are soft skills? Well, firstly, they aren't particularly soft. When I launched Ethical Angel the major focus of our solution was to develop what we called, 'power-skills'. A far more apt title I thought when we consider what 'soft skills' actually are and now I am reading about 'real skills' as well. But, to avoid exacerbating confusion I'll continue to use soft skills for now.

The Oxford Dictionary describes soft skills as, "*personal attributes that enable someone to interact effectively and harmoniously with other people*". This clearly encompasses a broad range of non-technical competencies such as critical thinking, communication, influencing etc. Going back to our story, Beatrice would appear to have mastered soft skills far more than Kalm. This represents a problem for employers, after all they need their people to interact, team-up and lead each other. A lack of soft skills will at best reduce efficiency and productivity in the workplace, and at worst result in tension and quarrelling. A 2018 LinkedIn study highlights the risk, "57% of leaders considered soft skills more crucial than hard skills"[cxvii]. So how do employers ensure that employees have the opportunity to develop them?

Historically, in the majority of cases they didn't, at least not directly. The workplace itself was the petri dish for communal social growth. The physical platform for social interfacing. Water cooler moments, office politics, Christmas parties, after-work drinks. A kaleidoscope of interactions, an arena of conflicts, a crucible for relationships. The office is a powerful tool for any employer to engineer an environment of experiential learning. Where employees can observe their colleagues and managers – learning by osmosis made possible by proximity, helping them to hone their soft skills. Or at least the soft skills that are valued such as negotiation and problem-solving. Traits less valued, such as being late, or inappropriately dressed can promptly be discouraged.

For junior employees like Kalm and Beatrice, the benefit of the office is stark. Not only is it a rude awakening to work life, but they can also benefit from observing experienced team members in action and receiving informal feedback or guidance. Beatrice would have flourished in this environment, and probably joined social clubs related to her employer. Kalm, would also have been able to surreptitiously learn from his workmates without exposing himself. Their senior colleagues, such as Kalm's manager, could also benefit from the opportunity from the induced closeness of the office as they support and mentor junior members of the team, developing leadership experience and skill sets in the process.

However, even the office alone wasn't sufficient alone. In 2016, Deloitte published its Global Human Capital Trends report. It highlighted that "92% of respondents believe that soft skills are a significant issue in their organisations"[cxviii]. Employers such as National Westminster Bank began to instil programs that included buddying up employees across different teams to develop collaboration and creating opportunities for critical thinking and leadership development among younger employees by encouraging them to shadow more experienced colleagues or executives. Encouraging steps, dramatically curtailed only a few years later when the Coronavirus pandemic struck and the office – that cornerstone for soft-skill development, was closed.

Or was it?

Certainly, in our story, the closing of the office because of COVID restrictions effected Kalm and Beatrice in different ways. Whilst Beatrice sought other opportunities, albeit virtually, for social interaction and networking, Kalm did not and quickly felt a bit lost, even isolated. His lack of confidence, at the thought of asking for help proved a challenge. Perhaps in an office environment it may have been less daunting. As Jonathan Eighteen says, "Covid has removed many of the intangible benefits of learning from others". A nudge and a whisper could have a colleague pointing him in the right direction.

But what about the generations of employees who've joined the workforce since? For most, the soft skills they've had to develop are for a virtual environment. As Steve Margison explained, "Environmental conditions change. When the environment forced people to behave in a different way, they did. It shapes our behaviours because we're continually adapting". This new generation is habituated to instantaneous, app-centric communication, which influences their expectations and behaviours in a professional setting. In this context the soft skills of greatest value could be argued as:

Digital Proficiency: New hires need to quickly grasp the digital tools the company uses for communication and collaboration. This involves more than just technical know-how; understanding digital etiquette is key.

Virtual Teamwork: With remote work, employees need to work effectively with colleagues across various locations and time zones. This calls for enhanced coordination and communication skills.

Self-Direction: Remote work often involves flexible schedules, necessitating the ability for new employees to manage their time efficiently, stay motivated, and work independently.

Digital Emotional Intelligence: Interpreting tone in digital communication, empathising with remote colleagues, and maintaining positive relationships become crucial when face-to-face interactions are limited.

Adaptability: New hires must be open to learning and quickly adapting to new tools, technologies, and resilient to new work practices, whether operating from home or meeting physically in the office to stay relevant and productive.

Cultural Awareness: As remote work often leads to diverse teams, new employees must respect and communicate effectively across different cultures. This awareness is vital for maintaining harmony within remote teams.

So, while traditional soft skills like communication, teamwork, and critical-thinking remain important, they are being reframed and expanded by the advent of 'new' and/or 'different' work practices and critically work environments. The challenge for workplace learning is for employers to manage this fluidity and incorporate these evolving skills into their training and development programs.

To provide a flexible, supportive learning environment

We've already considered the effects of changing environment on skills, let's now look at the importance of flexibility. In examining the impact of our evolving environment on skills, it's crucial to also underscore the significance of flexibility. The pandemic and the ensuing transition to remote work have accentuated not only the value of flexible learning in the workplace but also the necessity for well-crafted learning initiatives. As work hours and settings become more versatile, our learning approaches must similarly evolve to keep pace.

Employees increasingly seek learning resources accessible in a manner and timeframe suiting their individual circumstances. Consequently, learning modules must be architected to facilitate self-paced study. This flexibility isn't merely a convenient feature, but an essential aspect acknowledging the diverse schedules and responsibilities of modern workers, which often include balancing work tasks with personal commitments.

But it's crucial to recognise that flexibility doesn't automatically equate to remote learning. Consider those who thrive through osmosis or exposure to a shared physical environment. There's also a significant moral issue entwined with framing flexible learning solely within the context of remote working. Patrick Dunne asserts that conflating learning with remote work can unwittingly foster inequality. "I worry a lot about that," Dunne says, "We know that from the EY Foundation, that if you're from a family on free school meals, you're more likely to live house-mates of siblings and have limited to a private works space". The learning environment and how that is likely to lead to success, or not, needs to be considered. So when we think of flexibility in learning, what we should be thinking of is adaptability and inclusivity, not just the physical location or mode of learning. It's about reshaping learning to fit the needs of the learner, not the other way around.

Pretty straightforward stuff, but how about the second part of this the above title, "supportive learning environment". What does that mean, why do employees want it and how do they expect to experience it?

Creating a learning culture also means promoting voluntary participation in learning initiatives. A culture of learning is not about compelling employees to learn; instead, it's about fostering a love for learning and a curiosity for personal growth. "The underlying purpose should be that you value your people," says Professor Sawatzky. "When you value people, you build into them. If you find out what people are really good at and you help them to be better, there's something that happens with their overall confidence. You're telling them, I believe in you. I think you have a lot to offer this organisation." It's about presenting therefore, opportunities for advancement in an appealing manner that encourages proactive participation. Employees should feel excited about learning, not see it as a chore. But for many employees this is not the experience they will remember, even if it is available. Patrick Dunne explained, "At 3i, our culture enabled and encouraged people to explore learning opportunities, if they wanted to go to a conference irrespective of what it was on, then they could".

You'll recall we spoke about compliance training in the chapter on what employers need from their workplace learning programmes? The final part of the chapter says:

"Compliance training is compulsory, employees must accept education in it, therefore universal engagement is guaranteed."

For many employees, compliance training is their first brush with workplace learning. It's something that most employees will have to do several times over the course of their career. Its education in the truest sense, a strict syllabus with a clear measurable outcome. A juxtaposition to the personal act of learning and I strongly feel detrimental to ensuring a learning culture.

If we played out one of the examples of compliance training initiatives from earlier, say we are an employee at Siemens in the early 2000s. The company is in crisis. The regulator and the court of public opinion are deeply troubled by the apparent and flagrantly corrupt behaviour of certain staff members. Shareholders, up in arms as their stock price drops and are calling for immediate remedial action.

The board mandates that re-education is the solution. They inform the executive team, who in turn inform the heads of learning and human resources who build the appropriate training modules – outlining bribery, what it is and why not to do it... So far, so good. But, lets imagine that our characters from earlier, Kalm, Beatrice and Sophia were all working at Siemens during this period. Just three of the three hundred thousand employees employed by the company. Let's further assume that Kalm, Beatrice and Sophia are all at different levels, different divisions and in different countries. Yet, they are all obligated to take this training. Not just that, they need to renew it every year.

A few months later, the storm has largely blown over. The board have been seen to act and from their perspective, their re-education initiative is a success. The executive team is content, department heads are satisfied as they observe a 100% participation rate for their training modules. But how does this scenario resonate with the employees?

Kalm, Beatrice and Sophia aren't client facing, there is very little chance that they will ever be in a position where a bribe might be offered. Still, each time they log into the company's Learning Experience Platform, they're met with reminders about the pending compliance training. This reoccurring notice is not just disruptive, but also a source of irritation. As Adam Weisblatt of Blank Page Learning says, "If an employee is frustrated with the process of compliance training, then they will not be open to exploring more learning. If an employee values self-directed learning, they will bristle at mandated compliance training"[cxix].

Clearly, this experience is not conducive to fostering a learning culture – whereby employees are encouraged to seek out opportunities for personal development and growth. But employers do need to mitigate business risk whilst encouraging learning. So how could they instil a learning culture?

Well. Let's start with what a learning culture is. Essentially, a culture of learning is a culmination of shared values, practices, and behaviours that promotes continuous learning and growth among employees. It's an environment where curiosity and innovation are celebrated, and knowledge sharing becomes second nature. "Successful learning is about students learning how to learn and learning how to think," says Professor Roberta Sawatzky. "If people can learn about the things, they really are passionate about, they can roll over those skills to their daily tasks".

So, when we talk about fostering a learning culture, we're essentially discussing creating an atmosphere that encourages a growth mindset. This concept, first put forward by psychologist Carol Dweck, argues that intelligence can be developed and enhanced over time. Fostering this perspective sparks a passion for growth and learning, pushing us to soldier on through hurdles, eagerly absorb feedback, and celebrate when others thrive. This stands in stark contrast to the fixed mindset, where one believes intelligence is set in stone. Here, the focus is more on flaunting one's smarts rather than genuinely honing them, often resulting in dodging challenges, dismissing feedback, and holding back effort.

However, cultivating such a culture is not an overnight task. It's a gradual process that requires clear communication, commitment, and involvement from all levels of the organisation. Microsoft's CEO, Satya Nadella who was inspired by Dweck, "has spent the past few years focused on transforming Microsoft into a learn-it-all culture, believing that "the 'learn-it-all' perspective and growth mindest will always perform better" [cxx]. In this way, employees are encouraged to see challenges as opportunities for growth rather than insurmountable obstacles.

The importance of flexibility in a learning culture cannot be stressed enough. The pace of change in the modern world is staggering. The skills and knowledge that are relevant today may not hold the same value tomorrow. Hence, a learning culture should be adaptive, capable of evolving with changing times and individual learning needs. Part of the issue stems from the fact that learning and development is frequently depicted as a set of deadlines. Rather than focusing on what an employee can learn, the emphasis is on when certain courses are due for completion. This constrictive perspective hinders the learning process for a considerable segment of the workforce as individuals acquire new skills at varying paces and through diverse methods. For instance, Microsoft is shifting towards a more continuous rhythm that not only addresses deadlines but also informs employees about available learning resources and how these can benefit them both presently and in the future.

Lastly, creating a robust learning culture within an organisation requires more than just providing learning resources or opportunities. Two essential elements often overlooked in this process are safety and reflection.

Safety, in the context of a learning culture, means creating an environment where employees feel safe to take risks, make mistakes, and learn from them. As suggested by Amy C. Edmondson's theory of psychological safety, it's important that organisations acknowledge the inevitability of mistakes. In doing so, they afford employees the liberty to experiment and take risks, devoid of any fear of reprisals or humiliation. Edmondson says, "For knowledge work to flourish, the workplace must be one where people feel able to share their knowledge! This means sharing concerns, questions, mistakes, and half-formed ideas"[cxxi]. Such an approach fosters creative problem-solving, teamwork, and innovation — all fundamental elements to a thriving business. Outside formal training sessions, employees often turn to platforms like YouTube, books, and social media channels like TikTok – environments they feel safe - to expand their skills and knowledge. Such informal learning, driven by personal curiosity, can introduce novel insights and innovative approaches.

But, the best learning often happens when we step out of our comfort zones, which requires a certain degree of vulnerability. If an employee fears retribution or ridicule when they make a mistake or don't immediately grasp a new concept, their motivation to learn and grow will be severely dampened. Encouraging, therefore, a safe and non-judgmental learning environment fosters creativity, innovation, and encourages individuals to stretch their abilities.

On the other hand, reflection is an equally significant component of a learning culture. Reflection is the process of pausing to consider what we've learned, how we've grown, and how we can apply this knowledge moving forward. To see an example of how effective this can be, let's look at one of the highest performing teams in the world, the Royal Air Force Aerobatic Team or as they are more commonly known, "The Red Arrows".

The composition of the team is in a perpetual state of flux – each year newcomers join the ranks while seasoned veterans depart. Despite these annual shifts, every iteration of the team faces the same mandate: to push their machines, and themselves, to the utmost limits. The art of flying in dynamic, close-knit formations, at breathtaking speeds exceeding 640 mph, leaves little room for error.

And while the inherent risks have unfortunately resulted in some fatalities, they are startlingly few given the circumstances. Since 1965, amidst the backdrop of over 4900 high-octane performances, there have tragically been just ten. This prompts a crucial question: What strategies has the Red Arrows team adopted to uphold safety whilst still delivering on their squadron motto, éclat "brilliance" in synchronised aerial stunt shows?

Tom Westerling, is a L&D Portfolio & Strategy Lead for PWC. Tom recounts attending a Red Arrows debriefing after a practice performance by the team. He remembers:

"Following the practice sessions, the team go straight into debrief, reviewing the recording of the displays as a group.

This is really where the Red Arrows differentiate from other High Performing Teams. I don't think I have ever experienced an environment of trust, feedback and open communication quite like this before. As the team review the footage, they call out their own mistakes, faults and issues with the rest of the group. If required these are discussed in more detail and suggestions are made to rectify them immediately. I have never seen a process like it in business, there are no consequences for admitting fault, the only aim is to improve."
- Tom Westerling[cxxii]

Without time for reflection, learning is at risk of being merely superficial and certainly short-lived. It's a risk that the Red Arrows have learnt not to tolerate. By incorporating reflection into their learning process, the pilots can critically examine their experiences, gain insights, and develop a deeper understanding of their work and their growth areas. It fosters a culture of openness and trust. Critical ingredients for any team and any business. Critical for ensuring a learning culture.

In Summary

A survey taken by Forbes in 2019 found that barely 1 in 5 employees would actually recommend their company's workplace learning approach, whilst more than half said they would not recommend it at all[cxxiii]. When you combine that with the statistic from the same survey that more than 55% of employees say opportunities to learn and grow are more important to them than how much money they'll make at a job it is surely a call to change. "Lies, damned lies, and statistics" I hear you cry, well yes, you're not wrong. This is just one study, and warrants the same scepticism as attributed to Benjamin Disraeli. But, there is systemic noise we can't ignore. That there is a gap between employers' needs and what employees' wants.

We will conclude this chapter by summarising the employee desires I highlighted earlier:

Bridging the Gap Between Formal Education and Work: Like Beatrice and Kalm, many employees yearn for their workplace learning to reconcile the gap between their formal education and real-world demands. As Wilde quipped, the value of learning cannot merely be taught, a sentiment echoed by those finding their academic accolades insufficient for professional tasks. Owing to antiquated curricula, a focus on theory over practical skills, and scant academia-industry collaboration, they're often inadequately prepared for the dynamic needs of modern workplaces. Therefore, fostering a symbiotic academia-industry relationship is pivotal. As such, employees can blend academic theories with practical workplace knowledge, resulting in enriched learning and more effective leadership. It emphasizes the need for initiatives like internships, which provide valuable real-world exposure. Therefore, the key is not in choosing academia over industry or vice versa, but in harmonising them for a more holistic and industry-relevant educational approach. It's worth remembering, that "learning is a process and not an event" says Donald Clark.

Recognising Individuality: Workplace learning must consider individuality, recognising that employees are not a homogeneous group. Pedagogy and andragogy, two learning philosophies, can be used strategically to cater to different employee backgrounds. Pedagogy, a teacher-led approach, might work well for new recruits who have recently graduated and are used to structured learning. Andragogy, a learner-centric approach valuing experiences and self-directedness, suits those like Sophia, an experienced professional in the sector.

Historical biases such as the preference for extroverted employees can skew talent recognition and development. The danger lies in overlooking diverse talents who learn and contribute differently, such as Kalm. Organisations should refrain from pigeonholing employees into specific categories, ensuring learning and development opportunities cater to varying individual needs. Arguably, one of the positives of the pandemic is that people who might have never thought about being in a leadership position are able to consider that they might have something to offer if given the chance, and start actively seeking for the opportunity to get trained up in leadership skills to make an impact somewhere down the line. The trend towards greater acceptance of individuality necessitates employers to support all forms of diversity, across all levels of the organisation.

Cultivating Soft Skills in Myriad Ways: Employees today increasingly seek to develop soft skills, a crucial facet of professional growth that extends beyond technical knowledge. Notably, the evolving nature of the workplace necessitates a diversified approach to cultivating these skills. It's no longer sufficient for organisations to rely on traditional office environments to foster interaction and experiential learning.

The shift to remote work, brought on by recent global events, has emphasised the importance of skills tailored to a virtual environment. These include digital proficiency, virtual teamwork, self-direction, digital emotional intelligence, adaptability, and cultural awareness. These skills contribute to effective remote collaboration and the ability to navigate digital tools efficiently.

However, there's a challenge for employers to provide opportunities for their employees to hone these skills, utilising the best aspects of in-person and virtual learning. Therefore, it's vital for organisations to adapt their training and development programmes to address this gap, aligning their approach with the dynamic nature of the modern workforce.

Providing a Flexible, Supportive Learning Environment: Employees today seek a flexible approach to workplace learning, spurred on by shifts to remote working. They prefer self-paced, accessible learning opportunities. Moreover, in the most part they desire a supportive learning environment that fosters a culture of continuous learning and growth. Yes, there will always be employees who just want to be left to it. But this environment should encourage a growth mindset, where innovation and curiosity are welcomed.

However, cultivating a learning culture goes beyond simply offering resources. It necessitates providing a safe environment where employees can learn from their mistakes and encourages a culture of reflection. A successful learning culture thus combines flexibility, safety, reflection without fear and a focus on continuous improvement.

The factors listed above are not conclusive. To suggest that my musings on the subject are complete would be to fall foul of the same 'one-size-fits-all' approach that I've lampooned. At the end of the day, people are people, they, we are all different. But there are some commonalities that we can recognise to ensure that employees are given the opportunity to be engaged and productive at work.

Employees seek a dynamic, inclusive, and responsive approach to workplace learning. They yearn for a framework that bridges the gap between academic learning and the demands of their profession, effectively blending theoretical knowledge and practical experience. Where they can practice soft and technical skills safely, without fear of criticism or worse. An environment where individuality, far from being an obstacle, is a strength that learning environments should embrace. Such an ecosystem celebrates all forms of talent, encouraging even the less traditional ones to rise to leadership roles.

The future of workplace learning, then, lies in a culture that is diverse, inclusive, responsive, flexible, safe and supportive - one that values innovation, curiosity, and the continuous quest for improvement. Guy Stephens agrees with this prognosis but warns "The challenge/difficulty is that if you really look at this wish list of thinks, the perfect learning environment seems like an impossibility; that is the challenge!". It's time then to introduce the heroes of our story, those tasked with enacting this vision within the boundaries of employer limitations and requirements. ***Enter the practitioners.***

iv. The Practitioners

According to the U.S. Bureau of Labor Statistics, employment of training and development managers (which includes heads of learning and development) is projected to grow 7 percent from 2020 to 2030, faster than the average for all occupations.

Sandwiched between the tectonic plates of employee and employer requirements are the 'practitioners' with titles like *learning manager, Instructional Designer, Head of L&D* and *Employee Development Director*. Practitioners act like synovial fluid, both lubricating and cushioning the joint of workplace learning. As we've already explored from the history of learning chapter, their role has evolved in significance, driven by industrialisation and globalisation, advances in technology, and the importance of continuous learning in the modern era.

But as the breadth of their role has grown, so have the challenges. Expectations of practitioners in terms of what they should be delivering and how this is measured has continued to gain pace against a backdrop of rapidly changing workplace dynamics. Let me explain that. Historically, the expectations of learning practitioners was to ensure that the workforce could perform their roles. In the early days of structured learning and development for example, industrial age factories provided inhouse training of technical skills to ensure that workers could operate machinery efficiently. The advent of Human Resources in the 20th century required learning and development practitioners to be more holistic with their educational programmes, adding employee development to their existing technical-skill training remit. Towards the end of the century, the rapid pace of technological change, increased global competition and a more 'human centric' focus within workplaces meant that employers need employees who can not only adapt to new systems but also communicate, collaborate, and problem-solve effectively, with diverse teams across disparate working environments.

The exponentially increasing speed of change over this period looks retrospectively slow when compared to what happened during the Coronavirus pandemic. Almost overnight – everything underwent a seismic shift as the crisis ensued. In the workplace, the priority was introspective – ensuring that employees were supported to adapt and operate within these new conditions.

As Winston Churchill said, "Never waste a good crisis". Churchill wasn't being glib, but praising the formation of the United Nations in the aftermath of the Second World War. In the same vein, whilst COVID was a tragedy, it provided an opportunity for workplace learning practioners like never before.

"The pandemic has given us a real opportunity to step up and show leadership, to navigate organisations into the new world of learning and development. "[cxxiv]

To understand the pandemic's transformative effect on L&D practitioners, we must first recognise the catalyst that crisis provides for change within organisations. David K. Hurst's book, *Crisis & Renewal: Meeting the Challenge of Organisational Change* proposes that crises spur change - by shifting organisations from a fixed 'performance mode' to a flexible 'learning mode'.

In 'performance mode', organisations are structured systems where individuals perform specified tasks in exchange for remuneration. Conversely, 'learning mode' sees these individuals operating in more adaptable roles within teams and networks, with acknowledgement as the primary reward. Simply put, while the 'performance mode' is typically fixed, a crisis disrupts established beliefs, structures, and routines, thus spawning a transient, more adaptable 'in-between' organisation necessitating change[cxxv].

For practitioners, necessary change and rapid adoption enabled them to explore, test and expand new initiatives. To gain a seat at the table and demonstrate their craft. So what do practitioners want? What have they applied and what challenges are they facing?

Of late, a paradox has emerged in the sector: significant investment growth coincides with an increased scrutiny of learning initiative effectiveness. Could this be the fallout from the escalating tension between employer and employee interests, as we discussed earlier? Or is there more to the story? By delving into the heart of the issue, we might unearth a more effective strategy for successful workplace learning.

The Paradox

s workplace learning value for money? As a sector, employee learning and development has received increased investment as businesses grow teams and utilise new technologies to adapt to the challenges we've explored. A 2020, LinkedIn Learning Report highlights this pointing out that "global spending on corporate training rose by 14% compared to the previous year"[cxxvi] and the Asian Development Bank "ADB" reported a significant investment in human capital across Asia[cxxvii] and in In Australia, the 2019 Australian Workplace Learning Report found that 74% of organisations surveyed had increased their investment in L&D in the past year, and 84% planned to further increase their investment in the next 12 months[cxxviii]. This increased investment is replicated across the startup landscape, with EdTech startups such as Degreed and Guild Education able to benefit from increased investor interest in the sector and achieve multi-billion dollar valuation in the process.

At the same time as LinkedIn Learning published their 2020 report, Gartner revealed that only "only 45% of managers believed [learning and development] initiatives were effective in meeting business objectives". A study by McKinsey & Company in 2020, reported that only "12% of learners actually apply the skills they gain from corporate training programs to their jobs"[cxxix], suggesting that a large proportion of learning and development initiatives may be ineffective in driving practical outcomes in the workplace. In the UK, A more recent statistic comes from the "2021 State of Skills Report" by Degreed, which found that only 20% of the surveyed employees felt that the learning and development opportunities provided by their employers were helping them build the skills they needed for their jobs[cxxx]. This indicates that a significant portion of employees view L&D initiatives as ineffective in addressing their skill development needs. Furthermore, it is often challenging to establish a direct link between learning and development programmes and their impact on an organisation's success. A Deloitte report from 2019 stated that only 8% of organisations surveyed could demonstrate a clear correlation between L&D programmes and improved business performance. Asked why this was the case, Nick Shackleton-Jones says, "I don't think L&D is clear on its purpose". Several case studies illustrate the challenges faced by organisations in implementing effective L&D programs. For example, a large multinational company invested heavily in leadership development courses but found that employees were struggling to apply these newly acquired skills in the workplace. The issue, it turned out, was that the training focused too much on theoretical concepts without providing practical, hands-on experiences.

It's worth recognising however that this paradox is not being played out everywhere. Even the ubiquitousness of increased investment is being challenged. "There is much more of a budget then a return-on-investment mindset" say's Patrick Dunne, "Managers are thinking of L&D as a cost rather than a benefit". Dunne's assertion points out that managers often view L&D as an expense, not as a beneficial investment. This viewpoint highlights a budgetary approach, which focuses more on limiting expenditures to a specific financial plan rather than anticipating future growth. In contrast, an investment perspective approaches resource allocation strategically, with the aim of yielding profitable returns over time. So while the pot is increasing, is a budget or investment led approach? Is it looking for immediate value for money or a longer-term benefit?

There is even evidence that certain countries are faring better than others. In 2018, so pre the pandemic, the World Economic Forum ranked the effectiveness of vocational training and staff development in 140 countries[cxxxi]. The highest scoring countries were Germany, Denmark, The Netherlands, Switzerland and Singapore. The World Economic Forum report highlighted that in these countries they had long-standing traditions of apprenticeships, vocational training, and strong partnerships between businesses and educational institutions, which contribute to the success of their L&D initiatives. Omitting Singapore, the other link between these countries is the dominance of trade guilds and the Hanseatic League in their medieval history.

The problem, of desired outcomes not reflecting increased investment is likely linked to the amplified expectations placed on the shoulders of L&D practitioners. As Nick Shackelton-Jones, a renowned L&D expert, asserts that, "L&D teams actually perform multiple functions that are very different, and which require different approaches,". As we've seen, the expectations of L&D teams extend beyond basic skills training. They also undertake the critical tasks of cultivating company culture, promoting legislative compliance, fostering leadership attributes, and advancing strategic initiatives. The challenge for practitioners is that training the workforce to be compliant with the latest legislation requires a very different method to developing the character traits of future leaders. The greater their remit, the more diluted their focus and more marginal the gain.

At the highest level, it comes down to the core difference between learning and education that we explored at the beginning of this book:

education is an imposed structured system, whereas learning is the personally-driven acquisition of knowledge, skills, and competencies.

Most L&D programmes can be positioned within these two categories. For example, compliance training would sit within education and self-led character development in learning. But categorisation is the easy bit, implementation is significantly harder.

Let's start with compliance training. This is education in its most obvious way. A structured programme with clearly defined goals – such as completing an assessment to a certain level or certification and qualification by an independent body. Traditionally, this form of training has followed the experience of school education. A text-book defines the syllabus, and an instructor leads the training with an exam or test taken at the end of the period. This could range from a few hours to several months. Today, employees are more likely to experience compliance training from digitally accessible content libraries, with reams of videos and tests.

My first exposure of learning and development came in the first week of my first formal employment after graduating from university. Against the apprehension and excitement of joining the workforce and meeting my colleagues was the bland and mundane, 'watch and test' L&D experience. The importance of compliance training was made clear by my manager, but the sense was that this was just something you had to put up with. I'd login to the company intranet, then access my personal L&D hub, then mindlessly progress through the content, videos and interactive presentations (if lucky) before attempting the assessment. I will admit that I approached the training rather like the terms and conditions pop-up of any new product or online service. In other words, I'd whizz through it and click 'agree' or in the case of compliance training skip through the content and just attempt the quiz. After a few failings what I did learn, was that if I right-clicked on the webpage and viewed the source code I could see which answers resulted in a correct parameter. Effectively, I learnt that I could cheat, seamlessly secure successful outcomes and get bought drinks by my fellow graduates for also showing them how. Which with London prices being far more expensive than my Newcastle University student drinking experience was well received.

But therein lies the problem with the education approach, particularly of compliance. "We tend to force people into doing it, that's the biggest challenge," says Andrew Stotter-Brooks, VP of Learning and Development for Etihad Group. Whilst education and assessment is critical to employers, and they and the practitioners value the metrics generated by this approach – *x employees engaged, y completed assessment* etc. – as it shows clear return on investment it comes with a major setback. Like my first exposure of learning and development, for the employees the compulsory nature of compliance training paints the practitioners as the bad guy. Andrew continues with, "That makes it the most expensive thing you're doing with the least impact because you're making them do it. What is much more impactful is to turn on their desire, the want of the employee to learn. When they want to do something, they're unstoppable. The real battleground is trying to stop the blame game." In other words, if the employee experience of learning and development is initially negative that will affect engagement with other programmes, however well intentioned, enabling and personalised they are. Effectively, the practitioners has lost their audience before they've even really got started. Practitioners then face the immense challenge of winning their audience back.

If the educational approach is employer centric, then offering highly personalised learning opportunities is employee centric. Providing a personalised roadmap for each employee supported by a culture of self-led learning is the aspiration of many a practitioner. But clearly, delivering this at scale is expensive and worst of all, the return on investment is in most instances intangible.

I've previously referred to workplace learning practitioners as synovial fluid, cushioning the impact of colossal organisational forces. The comparison between learning leaders and synovial fluid is good one, if you'll excuse my smugness, because it beautifully captures the multifaceted role of these practitioners managing the needs of formidable organisational forces at work.

Synovial fluid does not merely cushion joints but also serves as a vital facilitator. It reduces friction, provides nutrients to cartilage, and removes waste from the bones, thus ensuring the smooth functioning and health of the joint. Similarly, workplace learning practitioners nourish the needs and aspirations of every workplace's tectonic forces; the employer and the employees. Ensuring the smooth operation of the organisation by providing the necessary 'nutrients' for learning and removing the 'waste' that could be bottlenecks or impediments to effective learning. They form a dynamic medium that allows the employer and employees to move and grow without friction, enabling harmony and productivity.

But, to consider our practitioners as solely cushioning agents, lubricating and enabling the smooth running of the organisational machine would be to underestimate the breadth and depth of their role. As we've seen in previous chapters, the significance and influence of their role has increased, buoyed by constantly evolving workplace practices and stakeholder expectations. Consequently, the learning leaders of today have shed the chrysalis confines of facilitators to emerge as strategic partners that have a role in influencing business decisions and outcomes.

So, the question arises: what do L&D practitioners truly aspire to achieve? Throughout my journey in researching this book and building businesses within this sector, I've had the unique opportunity to pose this question to numerous leaders in workplace learning. In the process, I have distilled a few key themes that provide insights into the goals and ambitions of practitioners.

Learning in the Flow of Work

t's perfectly normal for me, and maybe for you as well, to still be scrolling through my phone in bed, late into the evening. It was on one such occasion at the end of a particularly busy day, having finally put my phone down, I found myself thinking about the frantic nature of modern working life. I reflected on how amazing it was that'd we'd all become immune to the constant cacophony of alerts, notifications and requests emanating from our computers, tables, watches and phones. Technology promised us through time-saving efficiency, more opportunity for ourselves, for leisure and family. And, whilst technology has enabled us like never before I'd argue that we are more ensnared than ever before by the very machines we built to *serve* us.

The average workday is riddled with rapid-fire requests and a maelstrom of demands, from colleagues, managers and customers all demanding immediate attention and actioning. Our fingers dance a never-ending ballet - typing out responses, scheduling meetings, delegating tasks. Between messaging apps flashing with updates, emails breeding like rabbits in our inboxes, and phones that have metamorphosed into leash-like devices, we exist in a state of relentless vigilance.

So, how can employees find the time necessary for skill, competency and character development against the constant battle rhythm of work?

This challenge was identified by many of the workplace learning leaders I spoke with. That unending busyness leaves employees without the sense of tranquillity and space - the freedom to explore, the capacity to absorb, and the opportunity to apply that makes learning effective, if not possible. Or does it?

In 2018, Josh Bersin recognised this challenge and rather than fighting it sought to work with it. He coined the concept of 'Learning in the flow of work', encapsulating a new workplace learning approach that would incorporate employee development into everyday tasks and experiences. Bersin summarised the concept by saying that, "People now want to learn 'in the flow of work,' meaning learning is part of their job, not a separate activity" [cxxxii] . It is similar to ShuHaRi approach to apprenticeships that we explored earlier in the book. Where learning in not linear or transactional but a consequence of continued exposure and reflection.

It's easy to see why this concept would be attractive to learning leaders competing with the distractions and demands of today's workplaces. But, it requires a rethinking of how employees are educated and given opportunities, as Jonathan Eighteen, a Director of HR Consulting at Deloitte told me, "it's about opening the aperture away from the classroom to all of these other forms of development". At its heart, the learning in the flow of work philosophy is about ensuring that as an employee undertakes their daily activity, they have the tools to learn in real time the skills and to overcome any challenges they encounter. For example, an L&D manager might collaborate with team leaders to include learning objectives in team meetings or project reviews. Tools and technologies can be used to embed learning prompts and resources within work applications and platforms. The goal here is to minimise the disruption of the workday, enabling employees to learn without feeling like they are stepping away from their responsibilities. Paula West a director at NKD, goes further, highlighting the importance of flexible and accessible learning opportunities in retaining employees, "I think we should make it really accessible... learning can be anytime, anywhere. I think if they don't do that, they will lose employees". This sentiment is shared by Costas Kalisperas, an executive coach echoes this sentiment, "If [an employee] feels that their organisation is not offering them the opportunity to acquire the skills that will make them a better, more effective leader...first of all, it leads to demotivation and ultimately, potentially to attrition, people leaving". Learning in the flow of work then, doesn't just solve the issue of having to balance work tasks with learning but also is critical for retaining and engaging staff.

Central to Bersin's concept of learning in the flow of work are the notions of micro ad macro learning. Micro-learning's popularity grew from the crucible of two new technologies; learning experience platforms that were able to match a learner's requirements with a bite-size learning experiences in real-time and the accessibility of these environments whilst on the move with the development of the smart phones. The early experiences of microlearning were pretty straightforward and often just repackaged versions of existing eLearning courses. But, even these rudimentary applications showed promise in providing employees with the immediate learning they needed within what's become typical time-limitations and that they could apply what they learned more readily.

Micro-learning ensured a new paradigm in workplace learning of just-in-time training. With micro-learning the right information and training could be delivered and the point of need. For example, a employee grappling with a software application could access a quick tutorial and immediately resolve the problem, or a manager about to step into a challenging conversation could review a short video on conflict resolution.

Micro-learning can also be used to mitigate the forgetting curve, the natural decline of our memory retention. Information, skills, knowledge that we don't regularly use will get discarded – how many of us can remember how to complete the math equations we learnt in school or the names of all the chemical elements on the periodic table? In 1880, a Prussian psychologist pioneered studies in memory and particularly the effects of transience, "the process of forgetting that occurs with the passage of time"[cxxxiii]. He pioneered the forgetting curve and the spacing effect which argued, amongst others, that the best way to retain knowledge is through spaced repetition. Micro-learning can thus be used by workplace learning leaders to reinforce memory by providing bite size learning experiences at spaced intervals.

Macro-learning, micro-learnings' more contemplative sibling requires us to reflect on experiences. When given the opportunity, macro-learning gives employees the perspective and depth to grow and evolve in their roles. In Bersin's vision, the Micro and Macro twins don't compete for attention, but rather complement each other beautifully. Microlearning exits within our daily work activities, offering quick, practical insights that are immediately applicable. These micro-moments of learning form a network of steppingstones, guiding us through the frantic nature of work. Macro-learning, on the other hand, provides the depth and reflection we need to consolidate and comprehend the broader landscape – what it means to be good at our jobs and making sense of it all. Together, they embody the essence of learning in the flow of work.

The attraction for practitioners is that employees are enabled to learn in real-time, in the true context of their roles. But, as Bersin recognised the flow of work requires a balance of the two. Too much micro-learning, and employees can become isolated, blinkered and lose track of the bigger picture. Too much macro-learning, and employees could struggle to associate big-picture learning with their daily activities.

As compelling as "learning in the flow of work" might be it's come under some criticism. Gal Rimon, the Founder of Centrical (a learning experience platform) says, "it's little more than a fad or conversation topic among academics and management consultants, if it doesn't deliver results." [cxxxiv] Rimon's quote highlights the need for such an approach to show measurable outcomes in order to be deemed successful. And that's a problem. The majority of learning infrastructure utilised by practitioners was not designed for the task, "sadly, existing tech platforms twisted the concept without delivering on its promise"[cxxxv]. Essentially, software solutions like Learning Management Systems often fall short in capturing the experiential and tacit knowledge that underpins 'learning in the flow of work'. These systems typically focus on explicit knowledge that can be easily codified and standardised, rather than the nuanced, unspoken wisdom derived from hands-on experience and interaction. Therefore, LMSs may not fully facilitate this holistic learning approach, which values learning gleaned through real-time work experiences. Without observable improvements in performance, productivity, or knowledge retention, the concept risks being classified as an intriguing theory rather than an effective practice. Thus, for "learning in the flow of work" to be more than just a captivating concept, it must be complemented by strategies that ensure its implementation leads to discernible results.

Practicing, Coaching and Feedback:

Before becoming CEO of Ethical Angel, I had never managed a team, let alone a company. I'd never had any practice of dealing with tricky customers, navigating the nuanced landscape of employee management, balancing the expectations of investors with the reality of startup stewardship. By launching Ethical Angel, I had dived into the deep end and wow was I in for a shock. The realisation of my naivety as bracing as the North Sea in January.

The thing is, I had endeavoured to fortify myself for leadership. An array of books on the art of management and the spirit of entrepreneurship proudly decorated my shelves. Don't mistake me for a *Tsundoku*, (a Japanese term for one who amasses literature without getting round to reading it), let me assure you each book bore the marks of a fervent reader - dog-eared pages, notes scrawled in margins, and the accidental embellishment of coffee stains. I followed accomplished entrepreneurs via social media, consumed endless hours of YouTube videos on the subject, and gleaned what wisdom I could from networking events. Surely, I thought, I had done enough?

Yet, what soon dawned on me was that whilst theoretical immersion does provide a robust scaffolding, it's only through the relentless heat and hammering in the forge of practice that true understanding is shaped, and skills are tempered. The theory – the books, informal chats, videos - may provide the map, but practice is the journey that leads to the desired destination - mastery.

Practice, in essence, is the translator that converts abstract concepts into concrete action, allowing learners to adapt their newfound knowledge to real-life situations. Or, as Russian playwright Anton Chekhov put it, "Knowledge is of no value unless you put it into practice". But, practice takes time, and for a lot of employers and employees, time is something they are afraid to use it on practice, given how scarce time can become. We tend to forget that making mistakes and learning from them is a hallmark of education at its most granular point. If we don't give people the time and the space to practise, how will they ever get good at what they do?

"Trying and learning and failing is not allowed in most organisations," says Dr Burak Koyuncu. "Something has to be correct, planned, and applied already, and that doesn't give space to much real learning. How do we train entry-level people in making decisions? They don't build that muscle to make decisions until they become a senior leader, and by then they haven't been allowed to make decisions for fear they might mess up!"

It's an odd cycle we have gotten ourselves stuck in. We only want our employees doing the skills that they are absolutely, positively competent to perform. That's not the way the master taught the apprentice, was it? They watched, they learned, they started basic, and they added complexity.

"A lack of training and the room to practise can lead to impostor syndrome," Koyuncu says. "You might look like you're doing well, but you're not doing well. Some people from the 'in group' get promoted because they seem to have the right skills, but they know they haven't practised the right skills." It creates an odd culture of promoting people from within for no real reason than they were doing their previous job for a certain length of time deemed acceptable to be moved up the ladder.

The power of practice lies in its capacity to embed learning deeply within us, to make it an intrinsic part of our cognitive repertoire. When I shared my coming-of-age story with Dr Koyuncu he empathised, "When you are a leader, you have to make a lot more decisions. But how do you train people in making decisions? When they are entry level – they are not allowed to make and decisions, when they are mid-level, they might make some decisions. But it's only when they are leaders that they have to make a lot of decisions, but they haven't practiced". Practice, reinforces neural pathways, making recall and application easier and more efficient. We can see it in Charles Handy's quote: "By the time you leave this room... you will only remember 18% of what I had said to you, by the time you go to bed tonight it will be 5%... by the end of the week, you will just remember one idea. I on the other hand will remembered every single word that I have said.[cxxxvi]"

Without practice, newly acquired knowledge remains in a transitory state, however many books you read. And tips and tricks are susceptible to being forgotten. However, with consistent practice, learning becomes enduring, growing roots deep within our long-term memory.

Furthermore, practice is the arena where mistakes are not only inevitable but valuable. "We have this false belief that practice makes perfect, and that's not exactly true. Practice doesn't make perfect, but it does make better and it does provide growth and improvement", Professor Roberta Sawatzky reminded me. In a practice environment, we have a *sandbox* to test ideas and approaches without impacting real-life. Kalisperas recognises however, "It's quite difficult in a work environment to have a safe space where you basically make mistakes in a non-threatening environment, but it is possible". In the practice environment, errors can serve as powerful tutors, indicating areas of weakness and providing crucial insights for improvement. It offers a safe space where learners can stumble, falter, pick themselves up, and learn - iteratively refining their skills and enhancing their understanding.

However, practice isn't a solitary pursuit. If I picked up a golf club for the first time and hit a hundred balls a day, for a month I'd still be a terrible golfer, which I am. Practice thrives in a supportive environment where feedback loops are present, and coaching is available to guide the journey of development. As Sawatzky says, "unless there are clear guidelines laid out with clear desired outcomes, we could be practicing in such a way that improvement eludes us. So, the importance of skill or behavioural modelling is vital". This network of support ensures that practice is directed and purposeful, driving towards specific learning objectives.

Echoing this sentiment, Pamela Dow shares her experience of targeted practice and coaching from her time in the United Kingdom's Civil Service. Dow recalls stories of coaching in the Diplomatic Service, where the art of social interaction was taught and rehearsed. In doing so, staff members learned how to conduct themselves at social events, how to adopt a particular stance (think three sides of a square), maintaining a visible entry point for others to slip seamlessly into the conversation. This type of coaching was critical in ensuring that everyone, irrespective of their lived experience had the opportunity to flourish in the role. Dow says, "If you have benefited from [experiencing and learning social skills] throughout your life – if your family have brought you up with those skills, you don't know how privileged you are. The only way to make sure that the working-class kid who hasn't had that privilege can become an ambassador in the British Foreign and Commonwealth Office is to teach them!".

So, jump back to Ethical Angel, I'd been running the company for a few years and it was hard. Something was going wrong. Even though I regurgitated motivational quotes, brainstormed big ideas for future product development and discussed new-market expansion. There was a disconnect between my vision and the people I'd brought into the team. The problem, as you've probably guessed, was me. The solution, coaching and feedback.

When sharing this experience with Patrick Dunne, Chairperson of the EY Foundation and the author of Boards, he said, "Everywhere I have worked, I encourage leadership teams to get a coach". Coaching is often described as an art; it is a powerful tool to unlock an individual's potential to maximise their own performance. As every coach will say, everyone needs a coach. Most coaches have a coach. As Christine Caine, founder of Propel Women puts it, "To build a strong team, you must see someone else's strength as a complement to your weakness, and not a threat to your position or authority". Coaching, therefore is about encouraging employees to learn, rather than teaching them – a subtle, yet significant shift from a traditional *instruction* based approach. Here, the role of the coach is not merely to tell the learner what to do, but to help them discover their path to improvement, to foster self-discovery and self-awareness.

Yet, the art of coaching is incomplete without the science of feedback. Feedback acts as a mirror, reflecting an individual's strengths, areas for improvement, and potential blind spots. West recounted how when working "for a huge retail company many years ago, I had one particular boss who at the end of the week was always saying, "Guys, you're doing amazing, really amazing, really well done". I thought, Ok, you know, as a young employee, I'm doing a good job". West continues, "and then I had a new boss and the new boss at the end of the week would go, "Well, this is the one thing that you've done really well, but next time could you try doing this to make it even better". The two bosses were providing feedback, but one was generic whilst the other was specific. West concludes her story, "I learned far more with that second boss because they challenged me, stretched me with really adequate robust deep feedback". Costas Kalisperas is an executive coach and regularly works with leaders on the subject of feedback. Kalisperas says, "Feedback is the *Golden Nugget*. I mean, very few people are good at giving it", Kalisperas suggests a formula, "In order to give constructive feedback, you need to appreciate somebody in a ratio of 5 to 1. Five appreciations for every one bit of constructive feedback". In this way, feedback provides a sense of direction, aids in self-assessment, and assists individuals in making informed decisions about their growth path.

> *"Sending a really quick audio or video message to somebody and saying, I saw what you did. I heard you just took this training. I'm so glad that you took the time to do that. I'm here for you. Do you need any help with it? It takes how long to do that? Hit send and it's gone, but it makes all the difference in the world."* – Professor Roberta Sawatzky

Feedback propels the process of continuous learning. It's how we improve and within any organisation, whether that is the Civil Service or a multi-national corporation it is the bedrock upon which employees can learn, unlearn, and relearn. Adapting and evolving with the changing dynamics of the workplace. And more than just an evaluative measure, feedback, when given constructively, can inspire, motivate, and create a sense of belonging among the team members.

However, it's important to remember that the process of coaching and giving feedback is idiosyncratic. What I mean by that is as we noted right at the start of this book, what works for one person may not work for another, as every individual has their unique style of learning, their strengths, weaknesses, and motivations.

The practitioners I interviewed harboured a fervent desire to pave a unique journey of coaching and feedback for each employee, giving them the freedom to evolve in their own rhythm and arena. But of course, the cost in time, energy and money is entirely prohibitive to this ambition. For many organisations that seek to engage coaching and feedback into their workplaces the solution lies in the monolithic model of scalable standardisation. Prescribing the same modules, in the same sequence, to everyone irrespective of role or experience. This approach to coaching and feedback is built on the misguided notion that every individual commences their journey from an identical launchpad of knowledge, shares identical aspirations, and follows identical patterns of learning. In doing so, practitioners risk stepping into the same pitfalls as employers, futilely attempting to slot a square peg into a round hole. No degree of forceful persuasion can merge two incompatible elements, and the futile endeavour is bound to leave both parties bruised and battered in the process. In this way, a one-size-fits-all approach, it is not just ineffective but can also be counterproductive.

The American philosopher, educator, and popular author Mortimer J. Adler once said, "The purpose of learning is growth, and our minds, unlike our bodies, can continue growing as we continue to live." Coaching and feedback are the catalysts for this growth, facilitating the transformation of knowledge into wisdom, skills into expertise, and learners into leaders. By fostering a culture that values and implements effective coaching and feedback, employers can empower their employees to reach their highest potential and continuously learn and evolve, leading to overall organisational growth and success. The real conundrum that looms large, however, is striking a balance between this aspiration and its financial implications.

I think we can also bring in the iconic experiment by Ivan Pavlov, the Russian physiologist who discovered a fundamental concept that's still resonating today, especially in the realm of workplace learning. His work with dogs, where on ringing a bell food would appear demonstrated a simple yet powerful idea: a neutral stimulus, when paired with a meaningful one, can over time trigger a significant response on its own. In the case of the dogs, just the ringing of the bell would have them salivating. This idea, known as classical conditioning, has left a lasting imprint far beyond psychology and reaches into the way we can approach learning.

So, take a modern office. The hustle and bustle, the smell of Nescafe, and amidst it all, the opportunity for learning and growth. Just like Pavlov paired a bell with food to trigger a response from his dogs, workplace leaders can pair training sessions with positive reinforcements like positive feedback or recognition. Over time, the routine of training sessions can alone spark enthusiasm and engagement among employees, creating a culture of continuous learning and improvement. It's classical conditioning in action, right in the heart of our daily work.

The simplicity yet effectiveness of this concept is beautiful. By creating a rhythm of learning, paired with positive reinforcement, a conducive environment for professional growth is cultivated. Employees begin to associate learning with positive outcomes, much like Pavlov's dogs began to associate the ringing of a bell with food.

Specificity

When Scottish philosopher Thomas Reid said, "There is no greater impediment to the advancement of knowledge than the ambiguity of words" he struck at the heart of a paradox of human conversation, that the same words can generate a multitude of meanings. That the very linguistic tools, designed to make sense of our world and aid understanding, can often become literary stumbling blocks, obfuscating comprehension and learning.

No one can appreciate this sentiment more than the graduate employee lost in a thicket of jargon trying to make sense of business lingo. Remember Kalm and Beatrice (previous chapter) and how they were expected to get up and running with a technology application? I imagine that for them, staring at the knowledge guides and how-to tutorials felt rather more like decoding hieroglyphs than the continuation of a subject they'd been studying for the past three years.

For me personally, there is a particular irony in writing about this topic. Throughout my life, I've been accused of and often accept, that I've misused words or crafted sentences so obtuse that they are can only be misconstrued – you may have found some already? So, I recognise whole heartedly how linguistic ambiguity can derail the part of enlightenment into a spaghetti junction of uncertainty.

The workplace holds a particular challenge, here words are the invisible thread that weaves together the tasks, goals, conflicts and decisions of people. Which in turn determines the direction and pace of progress across the organisation. A lack of specificity here can lead to important messages getting lost in translation – of deals not getting completed, of the wrong ideas getting priority or even a media crisis. One example of this was when the American based breakfast chain, International House of Pancakes, "IHOP" announced it was changing its name to IHOB to recognise burgers being added to the menu. Investors and loyal customers were initially thrown into a frenzy at this surprise announcement. Fortunately for all, IHOP reinstated its name (admitting it had all been a publicity stunt) and managed to use humour to turn the crisis into a success by attracting new customers to their brand.

When Pamela Dow was designing the first ever curriculum for civil service knowledge and skills one of the problems she identified was a lack of specificity, "There is imprecision in how a job is defined, this is a problem in the civil service," she says. The problem with imprecision, especially in the job descriptions is it is then unclear what skills the candidate needs to have, and then as they progress through their career, what skills they need to develop. It's interesting to think about how this lack of specificity affects not just the hiring process, but the entire career trajectory of an individual. The ambiguity of words within the job description may result in attracting the wrong talent, and when these ill-suited individuals begin their roles, the lack of a precise, well-defined path can hinder their growth and trickle down onto others. This is not to say that job roles must be rigidly defined, far from it. Afterall, the workplace is constantly evolving and so roles demand a certain level of flexibility. But this flexibility should not be confused with ambiguity, particularly of skills. While the former promotes adaptability, the latter leads to uncertainty and confusion.

So, how does this all relate to workplace learning? Well, the next bit is going to be controversial. The cause of the problem, some believe, is Human Resources. As Dr Nigel Paine recounts, "My own experience at the BBC, the biggest fights we had was with the rest of HR", Nigel recounts a story of one HR leader admonishing him, "No one cares about your courses, what people want is HR staff, sitting with them solving their problems".

Indeed, workplace learning has its roots far before the advent of HR. However, the socio-economic transformations of the last century, which we've previously examined, spurred the rise and adoption of HR. Factors such as new legislation, globalisation, employee-centric workplace programmes, and transient workforces have all effected the velocity of its growth. To the extent, that workplace learning now commonly exists as a sub-department of human resources for many organisations.

But where is the problem? There is no doubt that the importance of HR has grown, as a reactionary and pre-emptive solution to the needs and risks of contemporary workplaces. But, I believe its meteoric development has given rise to a vocational dichotomic episode of imposter syndrome and confirmation bias that lends itself to the acceptance of questionable theories in the hunt for credibility. I'll break that down.

HR really came into its own in the latter half of the 20th Century, by the 1980s, the role of personnel departments had evolved significantly from primarily administrative and clerical tasks. The focus shifted towards understanding the legal implications and broader impacts of functions previously viewed as clerical, such as payroll and personnel record keeping. The responsibility expanded to help organisations effectively leveraging their human capital, shifting the function from administrative to strategic. Ruhal Dooley encapsulates this shift, noting "The world has gotten 'smaller'," he says. "The needs and expectations of society are ever rapidly changing. Human resources must strategize with businesses to anticipate change and adapt to change and to optimize the use of human capital within the labor force."[cxxxvii]

As HR took on the role of enforcers and their numbers grew, one issue is that more HR workers create more policy and consequently cause more employee transgression which requires more HR intervention. It's a perpetual circle, a self-fulfilling prophecy enshrined in Parkinson's Law, which states that 'work expands to fill the time available for its completion'. In this context, an influx of HR personnel could inadvertently lead to the creation of more policies. Consequently, this can increase the likelihood of employee policy breaches, thereby necessitating further HR intervention. Essentially, the growth in HR resources may be unintentionally contributing to an increase in the very issues they aim to resolve, creating a cycle that perpetuates the demand for their own services.

Another factor is that as HR grew in importance, a pseudoscience evolved around it. As a mixture of academics, practitioners and charlatans imparted and sold their research, experience and quackery on an audience wanting to believe in the science. This is where – at a vocational level – the imposter syndrome and confirmation bias had an effect. Science is credibility, when it is real science. As the Science Council defines it, "Science is the pursuit and application of knowledge and understanding of the natural and social world following a systematic methodology based on evidence"[cxxxviii]. One can appreciate therefore, why a department with an expanding remit and growing influence might gravitate towards theories and methodologies that validate its significance. As HR carved out a more substantial role within organisations, embracing strategies and approaches that endorse its widening influence can affirm its position and reinforce its contribution to the organisation's success.

All well and good unless the 'science' is more flat-earth then evolution. In 2019, Partick Vermeren, published *A Sceptic's Dictionary – The Good, the Bad and the Partially True*. "The book covers 55 theories employed in HR practice and it took Vermeren some 15 years to scrutinize all of them."[cxxxix] What Vermeren found was that of the 55 studied theories, 25 should be considered as pseudoscience, or "myths. "two illuminating examples are the DISC theory and the Myers-Briggs Type Indicator (MBTI), both aiming to create well working groups"[cxl].

If we agree with Vermeren's argument, that 45% of HR theories are lampooning as science then the scale of the problem is clear. As these inventions have through ongoing promotion have saturated every layer of the sector. From recent graduates to professional consultants, all inadvertently extolling pseudoscientific nonsense.

Now, let's circle back to the role of learning in this context. If HR leaders, while grappling with their expanding remit, are setting the learning objectives for their workforce based on the latest pseudoscience or trendy theories, it's a recipe for trouble. "L&D believes what [HR] tell them, *what we need is, these people have a deficit in… fix it!* And often they don't know what they are talking about" says Dr Nigel Paine. Vocational training in particular is a significant aspect that can suffer when the non-experts are calling the shots.

According to Dow, vocational training's crucial role is too important to be managed solely by HR departments. She maintains that the modern approach to HR, despite being well-intentioned, frequently undercuts the quality of Learning & Development initiatives, particularly in larger organisations. As such, reliance on fleeting trends or half-baked ideas can undermine the potential impact of these crucial development programs, skewing their focus and diluting their effectiveness. In this scenario, the careful balancing act between the ever-widening scope of HR and the need for high-quality, effective vocational training becomes increasingly precarious.

> *"Every single large organisation has seen this huge growth in people under this HR term. They are specialists in the field of HR but generalists, if that, in the roles and responsibilities of the actual job. Yet they are dictating what everyone does in their learning, it's bound to fail. The worst thing you can do for vocational skills and performance is give it to your HR people, it should be core business".* - Pamela Dow

Dow is adamant that for learning and development to be truly effective, especially in the realm of management, there's a need for clear, specific skills and knowledge requirements for each role. Abstract traits such as empathy, creativity, and collaboration, although essential, shouldn't be the primary focus. Even if they are the flavour of the month. Instead, these should be considered as beneficial by-products that naturally emerge from a strong, skills-focused learning culture.

To illustrate, consider the case of a leadership training programme. Rather than vague objectives like 'improve team collaboration,' tangible goals tied to specific behaviours or metrics, such as 'reduce team conflict by 20%,' or 'implement a weekly brainstorming session to foster creativity,' might be more effective.

Dow's perspective aligns with Steve Margison's viewpoint, who emphasises the importance of environmental specificity and behavioural exemplification. "Be very specific about what it is you want people to develop. So that means specific environment and examples of specific behaviour," he advises.

The role of clear communication in mitigating workplace ambiguity is also crucial. For instance, in a technology-oriented workplace, Kalm and Beatrice could have benefited immensely from a straightforward, jargon-free guide to their software applications. Similarly, civil service recruits would appreciate a clear and succinct description of their job roles, rather than a convoluted job description filled with buzzwords.

In essence, the focus should be on creating a comprehensive learning environment that prioritises specific, well-defined competencies and goals. This approach would counter the nebulous nature of certain learning programmes born of pseudoscientific theories and just might empower employees to navigate their professional development journey with a little more surety.

Learning Organisations and A Learning Culture

We touched on a learning culture earlier. But, it's a biggy in the goals of many of the practitioners I interviewed, and they aren't alone. In 2020, the CIPD's released their report, *Creating Learning Cultures: Assessing the evidence,* and "found that 98% of learning and development (L&D) practitioners wish to develop a positive culture for learning"[cxli]. The report goes on to say that only a minority feel like they've developed one.

So, what is a learning culture? How do you know if you've got one? Unfortunately, much as there are several explanations for the purpose of workplace learning, a learning culture is equally devoid of a unifying definition. Again, a lack of clarity muddies the water, and different stakeholders within the organisation will likely have varied views as to whether a *learning culture* is being achieved. Dunne, author of Boards warns, "the culture that's in the CEO's head is the dream and can sometimes be some distance from what the culture actually is".

What's more, there is significant interplay between the concepts of learning culture and organisational learning. The two terms are often used interchangeably and though interconnected represent distinct approaches. I don't doubt that there are many board rooms, who believe they are championing a learning culture when in fact the apparatus and processes they've implemented focus on organisational learning. Oops.

In order to understand why this matters let's do a quick appraisal of the differences. Organisational learning, "is a process of detecting and correcting error" [cxlii] on a collective, systemic basis. Chris Argyis, an American business theorist and professor emeritus at Harvard Business School goes on to explain that errors are any feature of knowledge or knowing that inhibits learning. Organisational learning is therefore about implementing changes in an organisation's knowledge base, routines and behaviours to enhance performance. Organisational learning is often associated with specific processes and structures that facilitate the acquisition and application of knowledge. For example, learning from a failed product launch.

Argyis, argued that most organisations employed 'single-loop learning'. In single-loop learning, organisations and their people take corrective action according to the difference between expected and reached outcomes. So, in our failed product launch example, the team having identified that something hasn't gone to plan would look to fix it.

A problem with this approach is that single-loop learning doesn't consider the root causes of the problem, only the symptoms. Perhaps, again looking at our failed product launch example, several members of the team were concerned or aware of potential issues that could jeopardise the launch. But even though they had regular check-ins they chose to stay schtum out of fear – perhaps the pressure from management was egregious – or their bonuses were tied into the product launch date. In this example, they apparatus of organisational learning, albeit suboptimal, existed. But, values necessary for the product team to feel they could share their concerns didn't exist, or were not sufficiently promoted.

"They have become frightened of being wrong. And we run our companies like this. We stigmatise mistakes. And we're now running national education systems where mistakes are the worst thing you can make. And the result is that we are educating people out of their creative capacities. Picasso once said this, he said that all children are born artists. The problem is to remain an artist as we grow up." - Sir Ken Robinson, Ted2006

Theories of organisational learning have developed over the years to combat this challenge. Chris Argyis and Donald Schön proposed 'double-loop learning', which requires critical reflection to correct underlying causes and assumptions behind problematic actions and behaviours. Peter Senge, an American systems scientist and lecture at MIT Sloan School of Management developed his notion of a learning organisation in his book, *The Fifth Discipline.*

In the book, Senge emphasises the importance of critical reflection, shared understanding, and systemic thinking in the learning process to affect change. Whilst Senge discusses learning organisation approaches, particularly around systems thinking – focussing on complex interactions and inter-group relationships as appose to the individual. Senge also identified the importance of the environment "People don't resist change. They resist being changed" [cxliii], which is closer to what we consider to be values associated with a learning culture.

A learning culture is the ensemble of values, norms, and practices that form the backbone of an organisation, encouraging and bolstering learning at every turn. It's about setting the stage where learning is not just an act, but the star of the show, valued, shared, and harnessed to elevate the performance of the entire troupe. A learning culture is therefore not just a nice idea, but a living, breathing entity, one that systemically infuses learning into every corner of an individual's, team's, and organisation's activities. Think of a murmuration of starlings bound by a collective consciousness reacting to opportunities and threats.

While organisational learning and the learning culture are separate concepts in the grand theatre of organisational development, they influence and support each other. Building a learning organisation is about creating the processes and actioning the systems necessary for change, for growth, for learning at a systemic level. It's the application of different theories of organisational management and knowledge sharing that gives an organisation the best chance to succeed. A learning culture however sets the stage, providing the social and psychological backdrop that supports and nurtures the dance of organisational learning. It sculpts the attitudes, behaviours, and interactions that choreograph the rhythm of the learning process.

But why does this matter? Why are our practitioners ambitious for this as a goal?

Reverting back to the aforementioned CIPD study we get a sense for what practitioners consider important with regards to instilling a learning culture, these are:

- *supporting individual learning and transformation and allowing this knowledge to shape strategy and process.*
- *encouraging teams to learn and reflect on their work and proactively influence strategy and process change.*
- *a willingness to learn and improve from the wider organisation and key decision-makers.*

What we can see is a theme of self-led learning. Supported by the values and systems of the organisation. For L&D practitioners, the significance of creating a robust learning culture extends beyond fostering an environment that values and promotes learning. It offers an opportunity to retain hard-fought for influence, and work to bridge the gap between the leaders of organisations and those tasked with embedding learning.

Too often, due to their proximity to the coal-face, the directives of learning objectives are set by middle managers or HR generalists, leaving L&D practitioners in a position where they must shape programs based on objectives that may lack the specificity needed for successful implementation. We've previously explored the influence of HR on L&D but let's touch upon middle managers. Firstly, I have great empathy for middle managers. It is a tough gig, balancing the objective goals of leadership with their subjective human resource. And, their job has certainly become more complex for all the thematic elements we've already covered. But how does this impact L&D?

Let's run a quick scenario. Chris is a middle manager; he leads a developer team, and his personal goals and bonus are tied to set targets for that year. Chris's job is to get his team to hit those targets, by *hook or by crook*. Chris notices an employee, Pete, struggling with a software platform and takes immediate action, deciding to send them on a coding course. Chris's intention is sound, he made a gut call and moved quickly, but the decision is made without a comprehensive understanding of the individual's actual needs and the broader L&D strategy. Remember the section on heuristics?

Consequently, Pete, a talented project manager whose struggles actually stem from time-management in a virtual setting rather than coding deficits, is inadvertently sidetracked. They find themselves spending weeks learning Python instead of focusing on honing their project management skills in a hybrid world. In this instance, Chris's well-meaning intervention becomes a stumbling block rather than a steppingstone to the employee's progress, not only frustrating Pete through distraction but also potentially contributing to mental health anxieties for being singled out and managed in this way. Such pitfalls underline the inherent risks of leaving L&D direction entirely in the hands of middle managers.

Building a learning culture, therefore, empowers L&D practitioners to stay attuned to the pulse of the organisation—the employees. As Dr Jac Fitz-Enz, explains that the key is to ensure employees, "feel that they are appreciated and that they belong. Developing this sense of community and a culture of continuous learning starts with finding the right people"[cxliv]. By promoting a learning culture, practitioners can support employees like Pete directly, advocating for their needs, and subsequently influence organisational leadership in future learning directions. And, this leads to other key benefits.

According to the Harvard Business Review, these include market leadership, increased productivity, and enhanced responsiveness to customer needs, according to the Harvard Business Review. Google's '20% time' initiative exemplifies the impact of a learning culture, having given birth to groundbreaking products such as Gmail and Google News.

In contrast, the absence of a thriving culture for learning can be damaging. Companies that neglect employee development often face higher turnover rates. As Simon Sinek warns, the lack of emotional investment leads to decreased contribution from the workforce. "Learning is not an activity that you do in isolation, it needs to be part of the way of working, they solve problems together – to solve problems they fail a few times and they then try again. but that culture of trying and failing is not allowed in most organisations. That doesn't give space for real learning" says Dr Burak Koyuncu, head of LHH leadership Development.

Furthering the emphasis on a thriving learning culture, it's notable that such an environment directly bolsters employee commitment. As highlighted by a LinkedIn study, a staggering 94% of employees would remain longer with companies that prioritise their growth and development. Therefore, nurturing a learning culture isn't just an added benefit; it's a strategic imperative for harnessing the true potential of an organisation's prime asset – its workforce. Echoing Peter Drucker's sentiment, "Culture eats strategy for breakfast," the strength of a learning culture often determines an organisation's trajectory and enduring success.

Dr Koyuncu, stresses the need for leaders to be "aware of creating that deliberate development of culture", understanding its substantial implications for both business success and societal impact. A continuous learning environment propels employee engagement and sustainability in business growth, But at what cost?

Return On Investment "ROI"

The premiss throughout this book is that workplace learning is valuable. That the benefit to employers of training up an efficient, engaged and compliant workforce is worth the cost, worth the investment. In the same vein, that if given the opportunity, employees can truly flourish. But can it be proven?

There is a reoccurring theme running through the book, a dichotomy between conceptual and human, the tangible and the intangible, the theoretical and the practical. This underscores a profound insight: so much of workplace learning, and indeed learning in general, operates in the realm of the immeasurable. "Quantifying the impact of learning programs is difficult because learning is a human process that results in intangible assets," says Dr. David Vance, Executive Director of the Center for Talent Reporting. Whilst we have explored a range of purposes for workplace learning and how in theory they make a difference, other than compliance as a litigation mitigation tool, it's hard to present a demonstrable argument for workplace learning's *value*. As the old adage goes, "You can't manage what you can't measure", and for the practitioners of workplace learning the great challenge is they are being tasked with measuring the immeasurable.

And this presents another problem. If, so much of workplace learning is opaque in its benefit, those who hold the purse strings will stop considering workplace learning as an investment – with a quantifiable return - and more as a cost. Patrick Dunne, author of *Boards* agrees with this sentiment, "over the last ten years, there's much more of a budget then a return-on-investment mindset. They're [employers] thinking about this this quarter's numbers, they're increasingly thinking about development as a cost rather than an investment".

There are those who have tried to develop mechanisms for workplace ROI. The emergence of strategic management in the 1950s heralded a new approach to workplaces; the importance of *setting objectives and measuring outcomes*. Key thinkers like Druker who we met earlier, introduced Management by Objectives, emphasising the need for high-level goals for organisations and their workforces to rally around, "an organization without clear goals is like a ship without a rudder"[cxlv], and Peter Selznick, who pioneered early concepts of SWOT analysis, examining a firm's internal and external dynamics. Other notables include Alfred Chandler, who underscored the necessity of a cohesive management strategy, coining "structure follows strategy"[cxlvi], and Igot Ansoff who expanded on these ideas and introduced gap analysis.

A contemporary of these *fathers* of modern business practices was Donald Kirkpatrick, who sought to codify the ethereal world of learning. In a series of articles, he introduced the Kirkpatrick Model, which proposed four levels of evaluation for workplace learning. "From its beginning, it was easily understood and became one of the most influential evaluation models impacting the field of HRD"[cxlvii]. The model is pretty simple and follows this plan:

1. **Reaction**: How did participants feel about the training?
2. **Learning**: To what extent did participants acquire the intended knowledge, skills, and attitudes?

3. **Behaviour**: To what extent did participants apply what they learned?
4. **Results**: What was the business impact of the training?

Whilst enduring, the Kirkpatrick Model has not been without its critiques. The overarching rebuttal is that the foundation to measurement is based primarily on the employees' reaction. And, according to Kevin Kruse, author of *Great Leaders Have No Rules,* "learners aren't experts in gap and need analysis. Learners aren't instructional designers. And learners aren't experts in learning theory and behaviour change… and here's the real kicker: learners typically enjoy the type of learning most that is least likely to change behaviour"[cxlviii]. The model's flow has also been considered problematic, "(1) The levels are arranged in ascending order of information provided. (2) The levels are causally linked. (3) The levels are positively intercorrelated"[cxlix].

But perhaps the greatest issue with the Kirkpatrick Model is the final level, **Results**, as linking specific training directly to business outcomes with absolute certainty is no small undertaking. Thorough analysis and expertise would be essential, inevitably escalating costs. If measurement is deemed difficult or seemingly impossible to assess, then practitioners may be more reluctant to do it. A report by Watershed, *Measuring the Business Impact of Learning in 2023* said, "only a select few organizations are prepared to throw the right level of resources at measuring learning's impact"[cl]. The Kirkpatrick Model will certainly deliver measurables, but whether they are the right ones or can be relied upon I will leave for you to decide.

Someone who thought they were lacking, was Dr Kack Phillips. Philips wanted an additional layer, recognising that, "to sanction large budgets, [employers] need to see the monetary actual value of these programs – their return on investment (ROI)"[cli]. This top layer focuses on comparing the monetary benefits of a program to its overall cost, typically expressed as a cost/benefit ratio.

Another enhancement on Kirkpatrick's model was the introduction of the *'Isolation'* concept by Phillips. His argument was that discerning the specific influence of training from a myriad of other factors affecting bottom-line outcomes was a significant challenge. "An important feature of the Dr. Phillips' evaluation model, therefore, is the recognition that credibility depends on the extent to which the evaluation accounts for these other factors"[clii]. This technique aimed to address that very perception, making the evaluation of training's business impact more precise.

Both the Kirkpatrick and Philips model rely on data collection, which entails choosing suitable methods, and determining the schedule for collecting outcomes data across different evaluation levels. "Depending on the nature of the training program, hard data (representing output, quality, cost, and time) or soft data (customer satisfaction and job satisfaction) may be collected in the course of the evaluation"[cliii]. While the approach to data collection has developed overtime, with the onset of the digital age, the underlying principle remains consistent. Follow-up surveys and questionnaires are employed to gauge stakeholder satisfaction and their reactions. On-the-job observations serve to monitor the actual application of the training. Tests and assessments offer insights into the depth of learning achieved, while interviews provide a qualitative understanding of participant reactions and how the program has been implemented on the ground. Focus groups delve into the practical application of the training in day-to-day tasks. Action plans not only foster the application of new skills but also chronicle the participants' progression and the tangible impacts observed. Additionally, monitoring business performance and scrutinising performance records and operational data becomes crucial to pinpoint areas of improvement.

A different approach came from Dr Jac Fitz-Enz who in 2010 published his book, *The new HR analytics: predicting the economic value of your company's human capital investments*. In the book, Fitz-Enz proposes the Learning Value Curve, a visualisation that depicts the growth of employees, and the factors affecting ROI over time. The model is interesting as it introduces some entirely new performance-based metrics, very different to the Kirkpatrick and Philips approaches. These are:

Timeliness of Measurement: Metrics are event-driven not bound by quarterly reporting.

Clarity & Practicality: A metric system that is easy to grasp for everyone, from top executives to associates. Fitz-Enz argues that overly intricate systems with irrelevant data collection procedures tend to fail.

High Leverage Points: A successful measurement system will prioritise fewer, but more impactful measures for maximum return on investment.

These principles bolster the idea of attributing a monetary value to workplace learning. Given the event-driven nature of the metrics, financial transitions can be precisely defined, allowing for both forecasting and validation of productivity. With clear and practical metrics, everyone in an organization can be involved in the evaluation process. For insight into the mindset of Fitz-Enz and why he approached ROI in this manner I share a clip from one of his interviews:

"I first became involved with HR, then called personnel and training, in 1969. I found a function that was regarded as a cost center that created no value. Having come from the sales and marketing side I couldn't accept that a company would support a nonvalue generating unit. So, I started working on a way to measure and evaluate in objective terms the work of HR." – Dr Jac Fitz-Enz

Now, I totally understand the interest in measuring workplace learning's ROI. But, surely if we get too ensnared in the pursuit of quantitative measures, we risk overlooking the qualitative richness of learning. Certainly, the outcomes of learning and development ventures extend beyond the obvious, often manifesting in subtle yet profound ways. Enhanced employee commitment, refined problem-solving prowess, and a workforce brimming with adaptability and innovation stand out as perks, even if they don't directly correlate with immediate financial gains. It's a sentiment echoed by numerous thought leaders and practitioners who caution against an over-reliance on metrics, or metrics that play to vanities rather than real value. "Increased engagement and improved innovation may not reflect immediately in quarterly reports, but they are vital for sustaining a company's competitive advantage in the long run", asserts Patti Phillips, President, and CEO of ROI Institute.

While quantifiable metrics are helpful, it's also essential to recognise that the most transformative learning moments might not always translate seamlessly into numbers. The profound shift in a manager's approach, the innovation sparked by a training session, or the collaborative spirit fostered through team-building exercises - how do we capture these in spreadsheets?

Part 3. The Future of Workplace Learning

W e've concluded our investigation into the past influences and contemporary demands on workplace learning. We've distinguished neuro-myths from neuroscience and categorised a glossary of terms and concepts. Explored philosophical and mercantile influences from different times and locations and the evolution of workplaces and workers. But, admittedly, our deep-dive has been more of a skim, researching and regurgitating the thoughts of others. Or as Oscar Wilde would quip "their thoughts are someone else's opinions, their lives a mimicry, their passions a quotation". We have only brushed the surface of this vast subject - a consequence of both my limited expertise and its sheer enormity. But have we done enough to answer: Workplace learning: Have we got it all wrong? I guess it's only fitting to share a fresh opinion of my own.

My belief is that in the majority of cases the effects of having multiple stakeholders, each with their own priorities, definitions of success and approaches stymies efficacy. There are outliers of course, or episodes where traditionally competing forces are complimentary to their organisation's overall purpose, "to help execute business strategy".

Being of a nautical disposition, the way I visualise it is in the art of rigging a great sailing ship, something straight out of the pages of a Patrick O'Brien novel.

The *purpose* of these great sailing ships was clear, to transport safely and effectively it's crew, passengers and stowage. "Few, today, can realise how important was the art of rigging a ship and reeving her gear in the days just old when all aloft was wood and hemp; or how great the part it has played in the building of Empire"[cliv]. Determining what to hang, how to set it and when really was an art, only made possible by a trained crew with a clear direction.

Rather like workplace learning, the topic is vast, it was an ever-evolving science, had a lexicon of terms alien to landlubbers and newbie sailors and ever at the disposition of the sea and weather. Even Captain George Biddlecombe R.N. author of the highly revered 1848 book *The Art of Rigging*, admits, "The very numerous articles and operations belong to the *Rigging of a Ship*, render it somewhat difficult to arrange this subject"[clv]. Yet, in the age of sail, these ships were able to traverse the globe, overcoming extraordinary challenges to deliver their purpose. Can we argue that workplace learning is doing the same for it's purpose today? I'm not convinced.

Within organisations, my feeling is that the *purpose* of workplace learning is not ubiquitously felt. Different stakeholders have different views on what workplace learning should be used for. Whether that be compliance training, development of personnel's vocational skills or even their morals and ethics. In isolation, those championing and leading these targeted programs may be highly successful, but as one practitioner tugs on a proverbial rope, another might unknowingly counteract their efforts. A program dedicated to diversity and inclusion for example may deliver targeted goals, but in doing so detrimentally effect the engagement of another.

As we've become more blinkered by specific problems or challenges of the day, the rigging of our ship has become more complicated. Lost in the isolation of the task in front of us, pulling on this, setting that, the purpose of it all is more distant then ever. Or, as in our employee case studies. Just as each member of the crew on a ship must understand both their individual role and the collective purpose, those involved in workplace learning must comprehend not only their discrete tasks but also the bigger picture. It's essential that everyone is on the same page, or rather, the same deck.

And herein lies the crux of the problem. I don't believe that every stakeholder knows the business strategy, their purpose, with the equivalent vehemence. Employers might bounce from one new program to the other, but as Nigel Paine says, "when will they ever understand that people don't care about their courses". As the calls from workplace learning change it's easy for stakeholders to lose sight of the broader horizon, focusing instead on the immediacy or short-term objectives of their tasks. And while it's crucial for every individual component to function efficiently, it's equally important that they work in concert.

We've forgotten the unifying purpose of workplace learning. Dr Burak Kol says, "Learning and development is still relevant. I think the form of learning development needs to change". Or as Donald Clark says, "Workplace learning has lost its way with its focus on values and Diversity Equality and Inclusion. It needs to return to competences".

Looking forward, is it possible to bring to bear the same level of efficiency to the complicated world of workplace learning? To ensure achievement of purpose?

Over the coming chapters we'll explore perhaps the most disruptive innovation to affect workplace learning, that of education technology. Before bringing everything back to argue for a new approach to workplace learning and the conclusion of our exploration.

v. The future's blue-light

"When it came near him, Scrooge bent down upon his knee; for in the very air through which this Spirit moved it seemed to scatter gloom and mystery. It was shrouded in a deep black garment, which concealed its head, its face, its form, and left nothing of it visible, save one outstretched hand." - Dickens

I said at the beginning of this book that our investigation would take the approach of Dickens' *Christmas Carol*, with the ghosts or past, present and future, to explore workplace learning. Dickens' ghost of Scrooge's future was the only one not to talk, as you can read from the quote above it was a mysterious, unclear impression of what was to come.

This is because predicting the future is just damn silly. The efforts people go to in aligning Nostradamus' prophecies with past events is only possible because of the cryptic, vague way in which he wrote. Other 'seers' such as Mark Faber, who's monthly newsletter, *Gloom, Doom and Boom Report* is regularly lambasted for its incorrect forecasts. As one trader said to him, "You've been saying the same thing essentially since 2012 and have been consistently wrong,"[clvi]. So, this chapter will be less a series of grand predictions, and more an opiniated appraisal of how new, but existing education or learning technologies can be used in the full recognition I could be totally wrong.

The first thing we need to recognise is that education technology is not a 21st Century invention. As Donald Clark says, "People think technology is new, but it has always been there." I cannot recommend

Donald's books enough for those interested in a far more detailed history of education technology. But, as a summary, we can consider oral communication and the written word as the genesis of edtech. According to the Old Testament, Moses educated his people by chiselling the Ten Commandments into stone and in the times of ancient Greece, "oratory and speech were the means by which people learned and passed on learning"[clvii]. Despite Socrates' famous disregard for the written word, we are fortunate that two of his students, the historian Xenophon and the philosopher Plato, recorded the most significant accounts of his life and philosophy.

Printing presses, radio, televisions and even the postal system made the consumption of education more accessible. Knowledge was increasingly democratised, with more and more opportunities for people to learn what they wanted to learn. As Eisenstein says: "Possibly no social revolution in European history is as fundamental as that which saw book learning (previously assigned to old men and monks) gradually become the focus of daily life during childhood, adolescence and early manhood... As a consumer of printed materials geared to a sequence of learning stages, the growing child was subjected to a different developmental process than was the medieval apprentice, ploughboy, novice or page."[clviii]

EdTech For Support

I f you do a simple Google search for EdTech, you get back 136 million results in about 0.76 seconds. So, we're not exactly hurting for solutions that have a technological tilt to them. But throwing technology at a problem has very rarely been the answer in any industry or for any problem, and doing so where the solution is so clearly people-centric makes it even less likely to be effective. A lot of times, a technological answer is the easiest one to put forth because it minimises our own effort. However, there are clear-cut limitations to what even the most sophisticated of technology can do, and the gap between its limitations and our own expectations is significant. It is fair to say that most businesses have an online or eLearning solution in place, and if they didn't, they swiftly upgraded during the pandemic when everyone was sent home and plenty have yet to come back.

As a sector, edtech is growing enormously year over year. The global edtech market was valued at US$85 billion in 2021 and is expected to move past US$230 billion in 2028. But if all that investment is going merely to be used for compliance purposes and to put together a huge library of content that most people aren't accessing very much, what in the world is the point of it? Ticking boxes? Taking quizzes? Demonstrating that they now are aware of how to report sexual harassment claims or what two-factor authorisation means? If edtech can't give L&D more than that, then we're failing from the word go to make a good investment in the future of our employees and the future of our companies.

And whilst we can tip our hat to the education technology of the past, the advent of the information age transformed the space forever. Our journey begins in an era where EdTech was simply a support system, a subsidiary player to traditional classroom settings. It was a place where platforms like Moodle, Blackboard, and Canvas provided e-learning solutions, supplementing face-to-face education. However, their inherent static nature made these tools little more than digital textbook counterparts, unable to provide the personalised, interactive learning experiences that students craved.

But not everyone was a fan, Richard E. Clark, quipped in 1983, that the new media "are mere vehicles that deliver instruction but do not influence students achievement any more than the truck that delivers our groceries causing changes in nutrition."[clix] . "The purpose of technology was not for consumption, but for production"[clx] says Kozma.

"Overall, if you look across the industry, the platforms are all LMS plus a little bit more, Bayer's Dr Ashwin Metha says. "LinkedIn and Coursera are great, but they don't go beyond their modules to the actual learning experience. They aren't involved in the part of learning knowledge that keys behavioural change. They are incapable of providing and evaluating experiences. Experiences are what changes behaviour and gives the opportunity to apply knowledge."

It appears that what is on offer is not really the problem so much as how it is being offered by the actual companies. "Edtech remains bounded by ignorance," says Nick Shackelton Jones, Founder of Shackleton Consulting and former CLO of Deloitte UK. "Rather like virtual homoeopath, no amount of technology can fix a bad idea. During the pandemic, we switched a lot of learning events to digital formats, and though this should have been fine in theory, in practise it was horrible for reasons no one quite understood. I have made criticism often, so I think it is only fair to say how learning technology should be worthy of the name: learning technology must matter to all of us and challenge us in ways that are meaningful. For example, a learning technology might know that you are interested in graphic design, and that a colleague, Susan, is a graphic designer with an interest in mentoring. It might spot a shared time slot and nudge you to ask if she might be able to help you. Learning is all about meaningful challenges. A learning technology sets personalised, meaningful challenges." In other words, while a lot of these companies can dazzle us with content, the motivation to access the content is lacking or non-existent.

Based on Jones' quote above, edtech seems to be falling short of the goal repeatedly and often spectacularly. The next wave of technology with an educational twist seems to be the coming of augmented reality and virtual reality (AR and VR) to give employees an entirely other-world experience in which to learn. Everybody seems to be talking up the metaverse, from Mark Zuckerberg on down the chain. The question for businesses is, do you double down on your investments for businesses and technology, joining META, and start bringing in the VR headsets. Is that what we want to do?

"People are latching onto virtual reality a little bit more now because that can start to give you the sense that you can actually practise some of this stuff," says Andrew Collier, Head of Learning at Campari. "But learning has to be that continuum of a bit of knowledge, a bit of feedback, a bit of practice, you know seeing what happens, learning from that, repeat, repeat, repeat, until you get better."

If people are already failing at person-to-person soft skills because they are stuck taking quiz after quiz on an interactive module concerning how to find what a customer's pain points are, is it going to get better when we strap a pair of VR goggles on that person and have them engage with a sort-of human looking avatar who goes through a series of permutations about the things they want in the product they are seeking to buy. Does it make more sense to go totally tech using AR-powered gloves and VR goggles than to pull ourselves back into the face-to-face world of small groups and seminars? No matter how advanced they are, the rules of tech are still limited. That's not an issue if you're trying to teach someone how to use Microsoft 360 because it's mostly commands and hotkeys. But what about when you're trying to read nuances of someone's vocabulary choices and body language when you meet them for coffee or talk to them over a Zoom call concerning a potential sale? We need meaningful opportunities to develop skill sets.

Let's take another dive into our narrative world to really focus on the gap between what technology can do and what real-life learning can do. This time, we'll visit with co-workers Barak and Lucy as they return to the office post-pandemic and get back to their jobs selling advertising slots for late-night television on a local TV channel.

Lucy is an introvert and thus COVID has been a little more pleasant for her than she'd prefer to let on. She worked from home, she contacted all of her potential clients via direct messenger and very occasionally did so via Zoom, keeping the camera off so they wouldn't notice that she was perpetually multi-tasking at the same time. Barak is a lot more of a people person and is always up for a sales call that spills into lunch, coffee, or basically anything that doesn't involve sitting in his cubicle all day. Both employees were newbies when the pandemic started and thus are in dire need of opportunity to learn their craft. The company they work offers them two options - to engage in an online training module on how to sell better to customers in person or to join the company's new mentorship project where a senior salesperson works alongside them to give them pointers, hints, and engage in one-to-one activities to strengthen their salesmanship.

For Lucy, the course is a no-brainer. She can dive right into the digital content whenever and wherever she wants to and go through it as quickly or slowly as she desires. Because she's got some coding in her background, she quickly figures out the algorithm of how the module is asking questions and what keywords and phrases she needs to look for in each section in order to ascertain the answer and get a passing grade. The practice sessions that she is supposed to do independently with another salesperson are time sensitive, so she merely waits 24 hours and clicks that she has completed the first one, then does the same thing for the second and third sessions. She makes a mental note to tell Barak to vouch for her if anyone in the company asks about the sessions, even though she doubts that they ever will. As long as she is in compliance with what they asked, she can go back to using her direct messages and texts to make inquiries and deals without having to bother actually speaking to other humans in real-time.

Barak sees technology as a tool to be used to make his job easier, not to do his job for him. The opportunity to get mentored by a senior salesperson is worth its weight in gold for him and he jumps at the opportunity to make it happen. The technical stuff that Lucy is concentrating on is just a drop in the bucket for Barak's mentor, who tells him that without the personal touch, you have to be pretty lucky to do well as a salesperson. He engages Barak in a host of different role-playing exercises, both sales related and in general, using his own lengthy experience taking on all kinds of different personality traits in clients to get the younger employee ready to take on the world. He even calls a few of his own clients to let Barak pick their brain on what appeals to them in a salesperson so Barak can craft his delivery to hit on those points. While Lucy is able to get sales from people who want the convenience of doing it all online, Barak is hitting up the clients who want to build a bond based on trust and customer service. You can guess who is going to be making larger and more consistent commissions and moving up swiftly through the sales ranks over the long term.

The problem then, might not be the system itself but the fact that we aren't doing enough around it to make it with our employees' while. "These (methods) often amount to little more than 'content dumping', and are largely disliked and almost entirely ineffective," says Shackleton-Jones. "We do this because we lack an understanding of learning, and instead substitute educational ritual and convention. People approach us with the expectation that we will do something that resembles school, in the belief that it will achieve a business outcome. Too often we do, almost always it doesn't. We are like superstitious folk who want to heal people, but have no idea how. We shake sticks and dance."

That is not to say it is not working at all, or the entire industry would be dying a slow, fiery death right now. But still there is plenty of conjecture of how much good edtech is doing, although clearly where you are and how committed your company is to the field has a lot to do with it.

Dr Ashwin Mehta of Bayer suggests measuring edtech's success really depends on where you are in the world and how important learning is for you. "If you think about adoption of edtech in the Western world, part of the problem might be that it's at our fingertips all the time and it's free, so it has less value," says Mehta. "In Africa and Asia, the value is a lot higher because there are a scarce number of opportunities. People see the opportunity to learn and think, 'I'll get promoted; I'll get a job elsewhere. I don't see that sense of motivation happening in the Western world."

That's a real lynch pin in our argument that the current technology is not enough. Even if you get great materials from somewhere like Coursera and you combine it with technology in the form of AR or VR simulations, you're still running into barriers that no technology can overcome. Learning how to make an in-person sales call to a new client who might be interested in your business seems like a pretty reasonable skill set to expect from a junior salesperson in your company, right? You hire someone with a business degree straight out of university and put them in front of the computer to go over the sales module before you allow them to go out into the world and try to make a sale. You don't want them to fail, so after they've completed the online module, you invest money in a VR sales training program that you've heard other executives talking about. Now your new salesperson is slipping on a pair of VR goggles and earphones an hour a day and getting an artificial look at engaging with multiple personas on his or her way to making a sale. The VR module is there to run your salesperson through different techniques, different types of customer personas, and forth. It's quite expensive, sort of realistic, and in terms of preparing the salesperson for the real world, a total waste of time. We don't need VR interactions to train our people, no matter how close to realistic they are. We are not at the point where any VR is going to be better than a flesh-and-blood human engaging a curious learner in a conversation, an interaction, a role-play, or a real-life attempt at learning.

"Experiential learning is underrated," Patrik Dunne says. "We're humans. There is a herd instinct to be with people we like and are comfortable with." While there's plenty of doom and gloom when we consider using edtech as the sole solution, plenty of companies are doing more and using it as one tool in the belt, not the Swiss Army knife. There are numerous instances where we can see where great edtech is being combined with innovative, forward-thinking companies to come up with real solutions for real people that garner real results Let's check out a few of those case studies to see what's really possible out there.

Case Study #1: Milking It

One of the largest dairy manufacturers in the world sells cheese, desserts, nutrition for infants, and dairy-based beverages to multiple European companies, as well as in Asia and Africa. Overall it exports its products to 100 countries, has offices in 32 of them and employs more than 20,000 people. The company uses its L&D department to enable its employees to attack challenges instead of reacting to them with the idea of constantly improving productivity and taking advantage of new opportunities. Prior to 2015, the L&D department for the company was decentralised. Some of its global locations had their own learning advisors while others did not. The majority of the L&D budget was spent on training the learning management system and identifying and amplifying the career path of individuals in the organisation labelled as having a high degree of potential. There was no overarching policy for L&D for the rest of the company. This led to multiple identified problems in the company including:

➤ No possible way to measure the impact or ROI of the program.
➤ A huge gap between the learning platform and actual job performance
➤ A model that broke employees into a class system of haves and have nots.
➤ No possibilities to invest in new technology, new courses, or any other sort of improvements.

The company solved its issues by redefining its role in the L&D process, becoming a creator of value for its employees over a three-year process that started by defining a new vision of what L&D should look like in the company and expanding it to include 24 projects inside its core business. It overhauled its organisational design and found new roles for professionals specifically focused on consulting, project management, and performance-based working. Each L&D business partner was paired with internal clients with the goal of one project per year per partner being completed. In addition to correcting compliance risks with poorly-trained employees, the company identified areas where human error based on a lack of skills was costing the company money. In one particular area where human error was causing frequent shutdowns in the company's packaging department, new L&D modules led to a savings of $140,000 in the first few weeks alone. Instead of training employees to react to shutdowns and stoppages, the company was training them to avoid them altogether, and saving huge amounts of time and money as a result.

Case Study #2: Off to the Academy

Santander UK is a financial services provider with 25 million customers and 23,000 employees. Battling financial crime is an uphill battle for most companies, particularly financial institutes who are having their security measures tested by cybercriminals and hackers every minute of every day of the year. Defensive measures work to a degree, but between AI-powered watchdogs and signs of trouble, being proactive to prevent financial crime is much more important than cleaning up the mess, particularly when it comes to your own customers' money. Santander, like most financial firms, has tried a lot of different measures to get its employees up to speed on anti-financial crime (AFC) to protect its customers and its own interests. But that has not been enough, because new threats come down the pipe quickly and it's tough to keep all employees trained on the same level and knowledge level in the bank to see AFC when it's happening, know the warning signs, and move to stop it. To this end, the company devised the Anti-Financial Crime Academy (AFCA) in 2020 to offer its employees both guidance and help to make sure they are at their best when it comes to fighting against financial criminals. The ambition for the academy was to have a consistent AFC curriculum in place with role-based learning experiences; to have an operating model combined with a governance structure that evolves the AFCA as threats get more complex and requirements react accordingly; make priorities of areas where the company has identified the largest margin of error between skill and need. The focus on the dynamic, interactive academy led to a 98% completion rate for sanctions modules and 89% of employees agreeing or strongly agreeing they would recommend the learning platform to their colleagues.

Case Study #3: Barchester United

Barchester Healthcare operates six hospitals and 240 care homes in the UK, employing 18,000 people. Like so many healthcare facilities, COVID-19 had a massive impact on Barchester, which left it missing staff members due to protocol. Even before COVID, Barchester had created a Workforce Committee, increased visibility at the board and senior management team levels, and made its career pathways more transparent to employees. During the pandemic, the company knew that recruiting would take a hit and that it would need to find numbers to handle the sheer volume of employees getting sick, taking leaves of absence or just leaving overall. It was able to convert all face-to-face learning to e-learning, adapt its digital platform to train more than 650 volunteers, accelerate the development of about 90 care workers who were in the mid-programme area of their careers, and develop smaller sequences of learning training for targeted employees to ensure they had the skills necessary to make decisions and remain confident around patients and co-workers during tough times. They also developed a programme for any senior care workers who wanted to step in and support the care facilities where they might have been shortages. Remarkably, the results led to almost no usage of agency staff care workers during COVID, a 10% decline in nurse turnover, and employee satisfaction rising to 85% from 72%. Quality of care as reported by an independent regulator, rose to 88.3% from 68.4% in the same time period.

The problem is that people are leaning way too far into EdTech as the only necessary component for solving L&D. Research, first-hand experience, talking to experts, and seeing the challenges all form to tell me that there's got to be a better way. Dr Ashwin Mehta believes that with more work in data, design, and methodologies, the day can come sooner rather than later where edtech is able to play a major role in helping companies figure out the best path to take forward towards mastery. "The thing about edtech is that we're trying to get a balance of this blend of push, pull, and share," Dr Mehta says. "We push the corporate training, we pull from a set of materials, and we share more knowledge from others. It's a difficult mix, but we could get there if we use data effectively."

A lack of ability to properly quantify L&D in data like so many companies have succeeded in doing with business components like marketing, supply chain, and various other Big Data-applicable business units is a vexing matter for those who believe that the power of numbers is absolute. Companies use Machine Learning (ML) to make close to real-time decisions on moving price points, rearranging where merchandise is displayed in a store, and figuring out which customers want to be marketed to via which channels and what times of day and just about every other criterion you could imagine.

But so far, L&D has continued to be the proverbial square peg / round hole conundrum. Possibly because people are much more complex in regards to their own career ambitions than even deciding what sort of product they would like to buy. Typically, the more intimate an emotional connection, the more likely it is to quantify with data. For many employees, embracing the culture of curiosity means peeing back layers of their emotional protection and allowing others to take a peek inside of what their true passion lies in. "A learning design is what is required," says Dr Mehta. "There are methodologies in many sectors that are being deployed where we can evaluate the findings. A likely shift is coming. Something equivalent to the Netflix experience of learning where you can get a personalised experience. It is a tough field because everyone is looking to find the new thing and add value. We can do some of it with recruitment, talent acquisition, leadership, and communication, but changing culture is not easy."

EdTech For Performance

E ducation technology offers promise, but it is not an all-encompassing solution. The development of new and innovate solutions such as large language models gives us another tool to use, but if misdirected, however *intelligent*, will be as useless as a chocolate teapot.

The essence of learning remains rooted in human experience, practice, and feedback. "Technology makes us believe we can do it quickly; it is too often seen as a silver bullet. But it needs more than that. Learning has to be that continuum of a bit of learning and a bit of practice" says Andrew Collier, "Learning is pretty basic at the end of the day, the challenge is executing it."

It's here that Benjamin Bloom's Two Sigma Problem becomes especially pertinent. The 2 Sigma problem was first introduced by educational psychologist Bloom in 1984. Bloom's research aimed to explore the variation in student performance when taught one-to-one or in a traditional classroom setting. The results were startling. Bloom found that the average student tutored one-to-one using mastery learning techniques performed two standard deviations (2 Sigma) better than students who learn via conventional instructional methods. This means that the average tutored student was above 98% of the students in the traditional class.

In the context of workplace learning, the 2 Sigma concept implies that personalised, one-on-one training could significantly enhance an employee's learning outcomes compared to traditional group training methods. The challenge, however, lies in replicating the 2 Sigma effect in a cost-effective manner.

1. **Personalised Learning:** The 2 Sigma concept underscores the importance of personalised learning. Every individual has unique learning needs and pace. Personalised learning strategies that cater to these unique needs can help employees grasp concepts better and faster.
2. **Mastery Learning:** The 2 Sigma concept also highlights the effectiveness of mastery learning, where an individual is expected to fully understand a topic before moving on to the next. This approach ensures a strong foundation and better overall understanding.
3. **One-on-One Training:** The traditional one-size-fits-all training approach is often ineffective. The 2 Sigma concept suggests that one-on-one training could significantly improve learning outcomes.

While the benefits of the 2 Sigma concept are clear, implementing it in the workplace poses several challenges. The most significant challenge is the cost and resources required for one-on-one training. It's not feasible for most organisations to provide individual tutors for each employee. Moreover, the time required for one-on-one training is another major constraint.

The advent of technology, particularly Artificial Intelligence (AI) and Machine Learning (ML), offers a potential solution to these challenges. AI-powered learning platforms can provide personalised learning experiences, adapt to an individual's learning pace, and ensure mastery learning. These platforms can simulate the one-on-one tutoring experience, thereby aiming to achieve the 2 Sigma effect in a cost-effective manner.

AI in workplace learning entails employing computer systems for tasks usually needing human intelligence like understanding language, recognising patterns, and problem-solving. These AI systems are capable of tailoring training programs to individual employee needs, offering personalised feedback and interventions.

A notable advantage of AI in workplace learning is its ability to personalise training. AI analyses employee performance and adjusts the training content and pace accordingly, potentially enhancing learning outcomes and work efficiency. Additionally, AI can ease the administrative burden on trainers by automating tasks like scheduling, allowing them to focus more on instruction and interaction with employees. It also provides insights into employees' learning, aiding trainers in identifying areas needing additional support.

However, integrating AI in workplace learning brings about ethical concerns, encompassing privacy, bias, and its impact on trainer-employee relations. There's also a risk of AI reinforcing existing workplace inequalities, especially if demographic data used by AI systems perpetuate biases. Thus, it's crucial to design and utilise AI in a manner that promotes equity, fairness, and a conducive learning environment in the workplace. As Dr Dale Allen, president and co-founder of DXtera Institute says, "AI in education can only grow at the speed of trust."[clxi]

The technological revolution in the educational sector has been a transformative journey, transitioning from a simple auxiliary function to a potent performance amplifier. This metamorphosis has been particularly profound in the realm of workplace learning, where the hurdles of scalability, customisation, and engagement have been long-standing. The inception of large language models (LLMs) such as OpenAI's GPT-4 has signalled a new epoch in this transformative journey, igniting enthusiasm and optimism about the potential of chatbot technology and generative AI to tackle these hurdles.

The excitement surrounding this technological revolution in learning can be attributed to the evolution of technology's role in education. As Sugata Mitra, an educational researcher, once said, "Schools as we know them are obsolete. I'm not saying they're broken. It's quite fashionable to say that the education system's broken. It's not broken. It's wonderfully constructed. It's just that we don't need it anymore. It's outdated."[clxii].

Historically, educational technology was perceived as an auxiliary aid, a support tool to facilitate the dissemination of learning content. However, the rise of AI and machine learning has significantly evolved this role. Today, technology is not merely a tool for content delivery; it is a performance amplifier, a facilitator of customised learning experiences, and a catalyst for innovation in pedagogical methodologies.

Generative AI has been particularly transformative. Unlike conventional AI models, which are trained to execute specific tasks, generative AI models can create new content. This capability has unlocked a plethora of possibilities for workplace learning. For instance, generative AI can generate personalised learning content, adapt learning pathways based on each learner's progress, and even create assessments to evaluate learning outcomes.

As Satya Nadella, the CEO of Microsoft, stated, "Bots are the new apps" [clxiii] . Chatbots can mimic human-like conversations, making learning more interactive and engaging. They can provide immediate feedback, answer queries, and even facilitate collaborative learning. Furthermore, chatbots can be available round the clock, making learning truly on-demand and accessible.

The enthusiasm around these technologies is not merely about their capabilities but also about their potential to tackle some of the enduring challenges in workplace learning. One of these challenges is the need for customisation. As Sir Ken Robinson, a renowned educationist, once said, "Education doesn't need to be reformed - it needs to be transformed. The key is not to standardise education, but to personalise it" [clxiv]. Every learner is unique, with their own learning styles, pace, and preferences. Traditional learning methodologies, whether classroom-based or online, often struggle to cater to this diversity. However, with generative AI and chatbot technology, personalised learning is no longer a far-fetched dream. These technologies can adapt to each learner's needs, providing a truly personalised learning experience.

Another challenge in workplace learning is engagement. As Elliot Masie, a learning technology expert, stated, "We need to bring learning to people instead of people to learning" [clxv]. Keeping learners engaged is crucial to ensure effective learning. However, this is often a challenge, particularly in the context of online learning. Here again, generative AI and chatbots can make a difference. By making learning interactive and conversational, these technologies can significantly enhance learner engagement.

The potential of these technologies to revolutionise workplace learning is immense. However, it's crucial to remember that technology is merely a tool. Its effectiveness ultimately depends on how it's utilised. Therefore, while we embrace these exciting developments, we must also focus on building the necessary skills and competencies to leverage them effectively. This includes understanding the technology, learning how to write for dialogic tools, and dealing with AI-aided design and curation.

I feel that the metamorphosis of educational technology from an auxiliary function to a performance amplifier is indeed encouraging, getting us closer to solving the challenge of Bloom's 2 Sigma Problem. With the inception of LLMs like OpenAI's GPT-4, the future of workplace learning looks promising. "ChatGPT, its performance support" explains Donald Clark, "we are now in the position of having technology, especially AI, that can deliver what Bloom called 'one-to-one learning"[clxvi]. However, to realise this promise, we must embrace the change, build the necessary skills, and most importantly, keep learning. As Alvin Toffler, a futurist and philosopher, once said, "The illiterate of the 21st century will not be those who cannot read and write, but those who cannot learn, unlearn, and relearn"[clxvii].

vi. In Conclusion

"Excellence is not an act, but a habit." - Aristotle

We've got there, thank you for bearing with me throughout this obsessive investigation. But what have we got to show for it? In penning the final chapter of Workplace Learning: Have we got it all wrong? I want to conclude with a candid reflection. My exhaustive and at times exhausting exploration leads me to affirm that we have, to a not insignificant degree, misconstrued workplace learning.

From the active guilds of Medieval Europe to the precise practices of Japanese kaizen, knowledge and skill have always played a crucial role in work. Throughout history and across different regions, the importance of honing skills and striving for betterment has been recognised. However, for all of its historic influences and champions, workplace learning is obfuscated, marginalised, and often the first casualty in budgetary trimming and the last to be considered in strategic planning. We've seen that the focus on continuous learning often gets overshadowed by the pursuit of immediate profits, what I call the paradox of ROI (Return on Investment).

The Paradox of ROI, for me, encapsulates the notion that a singular focus on ROI can lead to unintended or counterproductive outcomes. That the fiscal allure and accounting balance that ROI offers, overly narrows our gaze, blinkering our attention and naively simplifying outcomes. Encasing arguments in an uncompromising spreadsheet box that often sidelines the longer term benefits derived from less quantifiable initiatives such as workplace learning. For instance, an obsessive pursuit of ROI, particularly within the confines of annual or quarterly budgeting might lead to cuts in essential areas like research and development, training, or other long-term investments. To overlook the symbiotic relationship between an individual's development and the strategic trajectory of the company is to diminish learning to a mere convenience, vulnerable to the whims of fiscal austerity and the excesses of prosperity. Which could in turn hamper innovation, employee satisfaction, and ultimately, the organisation's long-term growth and competitiveness.

Workplace learning frameworks, largely unchanged since the industrial age, are ill-suited for today's technologically advanced landscape and workforce expectations. Spoon fed educational approaches, reminiscent of the Industrial Revolution's commodification of learning, no longer suffice. Instead, for workplace learning to be effective, it should not only align with rapid organisational changes but also actively support individual ambitions.

By applying an ROI measure, we subjugate workplace learning to a position it does not deserve, vulnerable to the whims of fiscal austerity and the excesses of prosperity. Instead, I propose a shift in our evaluative lens from ROI to Return on Interest (ROInterest). Unlike the former, ROInterest transcends the monetary dimensions, ushering in a broader perspective that places workplace learning at the very heart of organisational growth. It's not merely about the pounds and pence that flow into the coffers, but the intellectual vigour, the sparked curiosity, and the relentless pursuit of knowledge that empowers our workforce, fostering a culture of continuous improvement. By adopting ROInterest as our guiding metric, we are not just investing in the present, but are laying a robust foundation for a future replete with a well-versed, innovative workforce. It's about creating a thriving ecosystem within our organisation where learning is revered, knowledge is disseminated, and curiosity is rewarded.

So how can organisations go about building ROInterest to get Workplace Learning right?

I believe that at the heart of nurturing and embedding ROInterest in organisations lies the imperative of rendering learning both engaging and easily accessible. In my view, there are several avenues through which workplaces can realise this aspiration: delineating workplace learning from formal education, enhancing the accessibility and personalisation of workplace knowledge, and fostering a tradecraft mindset.

Let's start with splitting workplace education from learning. I fervently believe that the imparting of foundational knowledge, particularly in areas such as regulatory compliance, should be squarely within the domain of Human Resources, if it isn't already. It should be the purview of HR, not workplace learning, to steward the educational content that aligns with legal standards and organisational mandates. By doing so, they ensure that employees meet the essential criteria for competence and compliance, freeing up workplace learning to be something more expansive and aspirational. "People approach us with the expectation that we will do something that resembles school, in the belief that it will achieve a business outcome," says Nick Shackelton Jones. "Too often we do, almost always it doesn't".

But there is an opportunity here, as we saw in the previous chapter, to make access to this knowledge eminently more accessible and personalisable. Artificial intelligence tools such as Large Language Models, like Bard, OpenAI and even, there I say it, Interactive Tutor, can take huge amounts of information and make it conversational. There is even the potential for the knowledge to be 'pushed' to the employee at the optimal time, say that the AI can see the employee has a sales meeting tomorrow with a prospective partner, it could search it's collective data and send a timely notification to the employee with a list of helpful links, history of similar engagements and colleagues who could best advice on an optimal course of action.

What I am saying is that knowledge assimilation does not have to revolve around powerpoint presentations, videos and quizzes. It doesn't need to be boring. It could be far more emotive and useful, far more interesting to individuals. By doing so, organisations can ensure that employees meet the essential criteria for competence and compliance as directed by HR, freeing up workplace learning and it's practitioners to invoke something more expansive and aspirational. They can have the tools to help employees develop tradecraft.

So, in our new world we are utilising intent and technology to ensure a learner-centric experience of workplace education. Giving employees tools to take control over their development, avoiding as David Marquet says, "a vast untapped human potential is lost as a result of treating people as followers"[clxviii].

We understand that it takes more than dumping modules onto a server somewhere and telling our employees, "Knock yourselves out." We must create a framework that creates a culture of learning. Of creativity, as we've said before. A culture where people see their companies as being a means to pursue interests, whether they relate to their specific job function at the moment, or not. That's the first step, creation. Then we must educate our employees. Inspire them. Challenge them and create a safe space where they realise that their future employment is not predicated strictly on burrowing through course after course that will make them 3% better at their current job. We must construct a leadership in our company, made up of coaches and mentors, whose job it is to connect with employees, discuss what they want to learn about, and help shape a path to get them to add the skills that they want to, and hopefully, find ways to use those new skills professionally to increase their value to the company and their satisfaction with their role in the company.

"The form of L&D needs to change," says Dr Burak Koyuncu. "People can find knowledge anywhere. The training we run is usually about things people could learn on YouTube by themselves and that misses the point. We need to be facilitating learning, creating the environment for people to learn and try out new things." Many people say that they don't need to offer skills to learn because they hired people with the right skills already. If they don't see a direct link to overall strategy, they will not believe that workplace learning activities are going to lead to any real returns. "The next level is mindset because that drives behaviour. I don't think we are thinking about that as much as we should either," says Andrew Collier, Head of Learning at Campari. "What's the mindset behind the way business leaders operate? If we can change their behaviour and then solve a lot of our problems."

If we don't reward success or punish failure, nothing will ever change," says Steve Margison. "The environment will never change. We will become less agile and more rigid. If we're going to change our environment to help people develop their tradecraft, we have to be very specific about what we want to do. We have to be the leaders of the future of tradecraft. We need people to be more adaptable, because culture is a living thing that evolves." To see a good example of a created environment that allowed people to go out and learn through the power of collaboration, coaching, and curiosity, look no further than the race to find a cure for COVID-19 that launched within days of the coronavirus reaching pandemic level in the early spring of 2020.

Prior to the COVID-19 vaccine, the fastest time in which scientists had created a vaccine from viral sampling to the point of approval happened during the 1960s. The virus was mumps and it took scientists four years to produce the cure. No research company or government was willing to make any sort of guarantee about the length of time for a COVID-19 vaccination. Even optimistic guesses of something being ready by the summer of 2021, a full 18 months after the outbreak in China, were downplayed. Instead of doom and gloom, however, virologists and researchers raced to multiple vaccines during the fall of 2020, and on 2 December of that year, German pharmaceutical powerhouse Pfizer announced that it has developed the first immunisation to be approved for emergency use. Even with six extra decades of research and basically unlimited funding, the timeline was remarkably fast.

When I spoke to Steve Margison, he told me that there had been more advances in the virology environment in those 9-12 months than there had been in previous decades. The drug companies and academic think tanks broke the mould that they had all practised under previously in order to obtain something truly special, with the whole world watching. Namely, they stopped competing against one another and found common cause to collaborate, sharing ideas, opening lines of communication, and making staggering progress quickly as a result. Scientists didn't just share their knowledge and their expertise, they also shared things that normally would be closely guarded secrets like IP rights, actual materials, and technical infrastructure. They worked on trials together, thy had brainstorming sessions from all points of the world, they referenced each other as the expert on certain small niches rather than try to one up each other, and when someone experienced a breakthrough that put them closer to the end destination, they immediately shared it with everyone. It was like having 10 competitive rock climbers suddenly stop each time they reached a new height and continue to pull up everyone else to their current position. The rapid pace of advancement gave hope to the idea of future collaborations to more completely wipe out other diseases like malaria, tuberculosis, and the flu that continue to ravage parts of our global population every year. It didn't all come from scratch, either. Scientists had been researching other coronaviruses for years, aware that they might pose a threat down the line.

What does that mean for us as fans of workplace learning? First off, it should bring into sharp focus that the power of collaboration, particularly in the form of open communication with other people, is a powerful force that can move mountains and conquer seemingly impossible projects. It showcases how vital one-to-one knowledge transfer can be and how important real-life engagement and practice can be. Think about how many times different virologists failed to find the proper cure for COVID-19 during their rounds of research. They weren't booted from the project because they didn't find the answer. Rather, they were praised for the route they took, which could now either be cast aside as a false lead or used as a new floor to be built on as the collective kept pushing higher and higher.

Jonathan Eighteen, the EMEA L&D consultant at Deloitte, says some companies are starting to see the light and move in this direction on their own. "Talent and learning departments are beginning to take a proactive look by saying, 'You don't need a job title. There's much more opportunity for mobility, external/internal transfers, and talent growth," Eighteen says. "They are really starting to open the aperture away from the classroom/online module to explore larger levels of development, working on projects and working on scrum teams. They're going from using L&D for tidying the house to having a much broader aperture in skills to give employees the benefit of improving for themselves."

So, we can see this new paradigm shift coalescing through the testimony of our remarkable panel of experts, the hard data we have collected, and the simple knowledge of how important it is to learn from person to person with real-world experiences and the opportunity to reflect on them.

- Mastery of tradecraft needs to be focused upon, but not merely sitting in front of a screen making selections, nor strapping on the latest technology for some sort of near-realistic adventure.
- Learning needs to be pulled out of L&D and focused on from a deeply personal point of view that lasts over the entire course of someone's career with the company.
- The company itself must rebuild its culture to become one where learning is encouraged, celebrated, and rewarded. It must create an architecture separate from its existing HR department populated by some rough equivalent of wilderness guides who are equipped with a multitude of skills, the most important of which is the ability to act as coach, mentor, confidante, and facilitator for every employee who signs on with the company. The larger structure and the more personal coach will combine to understand what the employee is looking for at the company and in their professional development in general. The mindset of the company during this journey must be to embrace the employee's sense of curiosity, ambition, and exploration.
-

There are no wrong answers when a coach asks an employee, *"What do you want to learn about next?"* In fact, the only wrong answers are the employees who don't want to learn anything at all. They might be great at their current roles, but if they are uninterested in gaining additional knowledge, being flexible, and evolving along with the business world around them, a consideration of how long their career with the company will last must be made. For those who want to keep expanding their tradecraft, the company must be committed to helping them grow and actively looking for opportunities to use those new skills as part of their current positions, creating some sort of hybrid positions where they can contribute in multiple ways, or even an in-company transfer or the creation of a new position altogether that matches their new tradecraft mastery to needs that the company has now or in the future. For it's the future that we're really talking about when it comes to L&D - how do we continue to develop our employees to contribute to our future success as well as their own?

In both the business realm and the traditional classroom, the education is only as good as the educator. "We have an overemphasis on competencies and compliance and an underinvestment on character," says Patrick Dunne, author of *Boards* and chairperson of the EY Foundation, "We've moved away from recruiting people because of their character and instead are recruiting them because of their skill set. That's partially technology driven, because now we're in the mindset of 'we need this tomorrow, can you do it?' We should be recruiting people that have character with the knowledge that we can give them the skills and help them develop over a long time."

Within this environment we can also reimagine relationships between managers and their team. An argument for making them more omni-directional is shared by Andrew Stotter-Brooks, as VP of Learning and Development for Etihad Group, explained the foundational point of this type of learning. "As an airline we've completely changed the way we go about getting our pilots to coach one another," Stotter-Brooks says. "Traditionally, it's an interesting concept because a lot of airlines just go through a checklist that's one big file of making sure everything is going the right way pre-flight and during the flight and all the way through the flight until the end. What we've tried to do differently is have the pilots put the checklist aside, look out the window, and the two pilots have a conversation. They'll ask each other, what are the risks of the take off? What is the wind speed? What are the hazards? If certain conditions occur, what will you do? If something dramatic turns up, how will you react? And it's just a conversation, not a flight simulator or sending guys on a plane out into a terrible storm."

Stotter-Brooks' airline work stemmed directly from one of the most tragic events in aviation history. It was a perfect storm of events that led to the disastrous crash of March 27, 1977, when two 747s collided on the runway of Los Rodeos Airport in the Spanish island of Tenerife. The airport was seeing an unusual amount of traffic because of a bomb that had been set off at Gran Canaria Airport located two hours away on the same island. With so many planes in such a small airfield, parked airliners were blocking the taxiway and forcing planes to taxi on the runway instead. Foggy weather on the morning of the incident made visibility difficult for both pilots and the control tower. Neither plane - KLM Flight 4805 nor Pan Am Flight 1736 was supposed to land at that airport on that day but due to the bomb both wound up there. The KLM flight suffered miscommunications with the tower, and between the captain and his first officer. While the first officer questioned whether they had actually been cleared for take-off by the tower, the captain interrupted him and said, "We're going." Radio interference that hampered the flight tower's ability to communicate with both planes along with the dense fog. The KLM plane took off seconds before colliding with the parked Pan Am plane. Everyone on board the KLM flight died when its fuel tank exploded into a fire that wouldn't be put out for hours. Sixty-one survivors made it off the Pan Am plane with their lives, likely because they were sitting forward of the collision. The captain of the KLM flight was the airline's chief of flight training and one of the most senior pilots. He was so well respected and so associated with air safety that the initial response from KLM was to call him in to help with the investigation, unaware that he was the pilot who had caused the accident. Five hundred and eighty-three passengers and crew died as a result.

> *"The accident only happened because the captain had a false impression that he was a master pilot, the first officer challenged him on taking off and he ignored it. The expert isn't always the expert and needs to re-evaluate. Let's learn from the environment, not from manuals and checklists and guides. Let's discuss the potential hazards. Coaching is a much more important thing than ticking off boxes on a page."* - Stotter-Brooks

The attitude that we need is the basis for the culture that companies must create to be successful at L&D. It's not just about getting our employees enthusiastic about learning, but rather getting everyone on board the train to education-ville. Our leaders must share in the excitement of the ability of a company to transform itself through experiential learning.

"There has to be a changing mindset," says Dr Ashwin Mehta, Head of Global Learning Technologies at Bayer. "But changing culture is a difficult thing, especially organisational culture. You have to think about the culture of curiosity. A lot of organisations will try and say if we train people, we're good. But that kind of ignores the individual variation. Not everyone is the same, and that is what the rich tapestry that makes up our culture is all about. We are ignoring individual variation. We have to realise that different people are going to be reaching for different opportunities."

A major flaw in the top-down belief of corporate culture is the idea that every employee just naturally wants to learn everything about the position they are in so that they can do it better and make the company happier. Let's face it, a lot of our employees are doing their current job because … it's a job!

Everyone is at a different position in their life, everyone has different career ambitions, and everyone is using the job they are in right now for something. The idea that everyone that works for the company is only motivated to make the company better is antiquated and unrealistic. We have to understand our employees' wants and needs in order to get the best out of them.

The pursuit of education in the workplace is, in essence, the pursuit of excellence for the company. After all, a company is nothing if not the sum of its parts — the people within. To elevate each individual is to elevate the collective. Hence, it is imperative, not merely advisable, that learning be intertwined with our strategic aims. To address the titular question of this book: *Have we got workplace learning all wrong?* The evidence I have laid out suggests unequivocally that we have. Yet, acknowledging this is the first step towards rectification. We are presented with an invaluable opportunity to correct our trajectory, to re-establish learning as a critical, dynamic component of our modus operandi, firmly embedded in our strategic vision and treated with the seriousness it unequivocally deserves as an imperative for both personal and collective progress.

End Notes

[i] read, A.S. • 5 min (2019). The Top 10 E-Learning Challenges L&D Pros Face Every Day. [online] Docebo. Available at: https://www.docebo.com/learning-network/blog/elearning-challenges/.

[ii] Lee Hecht Harrison. (2021). The Future is Now: Insights into how to address today's talent shortage.

[iii] Frank, P. (2007). Einstein - his life and times. Read Books.

[iv] Chickering, Arthur W. and Ehrmann Stephen C. (1996), "Implementing the Seven Principles: Technology as Lever," AAHE Bulletin, October, pp. 3-6

[v] Mary Helen Immordino-Yang (2016). Emotions, learning, and the brain : exploring the educational implications of affective neuroscience. New York: W.W. Norton & Company

[vi] www.kentscientific.com. (n.d.). The Evolution of Neuroscience | KentConnects Blog Post

[vii] Thalheimer, W. PhD (2006). Spacing Learning Events Over Time: What the Research Says.

[viii] Harry Bahrick & Lynda Hall (2005,) quoted in the Journal of Memory and Language

[ix] Belief in Learning Styles Myth May Be Detrimental. (2019). https://www.apa.org.

[x] Fleming, N., and Baume, D. (2006) Learning Styles Again: VARKing up the right tree!, Educational Developments, SEDA

[xi] Scott Barry Kaufman, (2012), The Pesky Persistence of Labels | Psychology Today United Kingdom

[xii] TEDx Talks (2015). Learning styles & the importance of critical self-reflection | Tesia Marshik | TEDxUWLaCrosse. YouTube. Available at: https://www.youtube.com/watch?v=855Now8h5Rs.

[xiii] Zwaagstra, M. (2022). 'Learning styles' myth damaging our education system: op-ed.

[xiv] Fleming, N., and Baume, D. (2006) Learning Styles Again: VARKing up the right tree!, Educational Developments, SEDA Ltd, Issue 7.4, Nov. 2006, p4-7.

[xv] https://www.britannica.com/science/confirmation-bias

xvi Kahneman, D. (2011). Thinking, Fast and Slow. New York: Farrar, Straus and Giroux. Pg. 81

xvii Carl Hendrick (2021) The evidence is clear: learning styles theory doesn't work | Aeon Essays.

xviii TEDx Talks (2015). Learning styles & the importance of critical self-reflection | Tesia Marshik | TEDxUWLaCrosse. YouTube. Available at: https://www.youtube.com/watch?v=855Now8h5Rs.

xix McKay, S. (2020). The creative-right vs analytical-left brain myth: debunked! [online] Dr Sarah McKay.

xx Nielsen JA, Zielinski BA, Ferguson MA, Lainhart JE, Anderson JS (2013) An Evaluation of the Left-Brain vs. Right-Brain Hypothesis with Resting State Functional Connectivity Magnetic Resonance Imaging. PLoS ONE 8(8): e71275. https://doi.org/10.1371/journal.pone.0071275

xxi Mousa Masadeh, PhD, TRAINING, EDUCATION, DEVELOPMENT AND LEARNING: WHAT IS THE DIFFERENCE?, European Scientific Journal

xxii Habitly. (2018). What are 'Soft Skills' and Why Are They Important?

xxiii Defense Technical Information Center (1973). DTIC ADA099612: CONARC Soft Skills Training Conference.

xxiv Defense Technical Information Center (1973). DTIC ADA099612: CONARC Soft Skills Training Conference.

xxv Godin, S. (2020). Let's stop calling them 'soft skills'

xxvi Defense Technical Information Center (1973). DTIC ADA099612: CONARC Soft Skills Training Conference.

xxvii Aristotle, Nicomachean Ethics, and Politics, in The Complete Works of Aristotle, J. Barnes (ed.), 2 vols, Princeton, NJ: Princeton University Press, 1984.

xxviii Blumberg, Y. (2017). How a 2,000-year-old lesson from Aristotle can help you succeed at work

xxix Hartman, E.M. (2007). Socratic Questions and Aristotelian Answers: A Virtue-Based Approach to Business Ethics

xxx Stillman, J. (2017). Why Success Depends More on Personality Than Intelligence.

xxxi https://www.td.org/

xxxii https://www.cipd.org/en/

xxxiii Paine, N. (2014). The Learning Challenge : Dealing with Technology, Innovation and Change in Learning and Development. London: Kogan Page·

xxxiv UCL (2006). Novelty aids learning

xxxv Zondervan (2022). NRSVue, Holy Bible. Grand Rapids: Zondervan

xxxvi Encyclopedia Britannica. (n.d.). History of Europe - Growth and innovation.

xxxvii Jeter, C., Bedwood, D., Atkinson, N., Bruner, J. and Ford, M. (n.d.). Takumi: A 60,000 Hour Story On the Survival of Human Craft

xxxviii William Bosshardt and Jane S. Lopus (2013) Business in the Middle Ages: What Was the Role of Guilds?, Social Education 77(2), pp 64–67

xxxix William Bosshardt and Jane S. Lopus (2013) Business in the Middle Ages:

What Was the Role of Guilds?, Social Education 77(2), pp 64–67

xl Mirza-Davies, J. (2015). A short history of apprenticeships in England: from medieval craft guilds to the twenty-first century. commonslibrary.parliament.uk

xli Charles More, Skills and the English Working Class, Croom Helm, 1980, p41

xlii Ogilvie, Sheilagh. The European Guilds: an Economic Analysis. Princeton University Press, 2019.

xliii Malcolm Gladwell (2008). "Outliers: The Story of Success", p.31, Hachette UK

xliv Caplan, B. (2019). The Case against Education. Princeton University Press.

xlv Public, D.H. in (2019). 'Experience doesn't pay the bills': a lesson from medieval England. [online] Doing History in Public. Available at: https://doinghistoryinpublic.org/2019/08/27/experience-doesnt-pay-the-bills-a-lesson-from-medieval-england/ [Accessed 29 May 2023].

xlvi Bathija, Sahil (2021) "Inclusion and Exclusion in Medieval European Craft Guilds.," SUURJ: Seattle University Undergraduate Research Journal: Vol. 5 , Article 8.

xlvii "madrasah | Origin and meaning of madrasah by Online Etymology Dictionary". www.etymonline.com.

xlviii Ibn Batuta (1829). The Travels of Ibn Batūta.

xlix https://www.helpguide.org/articles/mental-health/emotional-intelligence-eq

l "Avicenna (Ibn Sina)". Internet Encyclopedia of Philosophy.

li Borhani Nejad, M., Rashidi, M. and Oloumi, M.M. (2013). Avicenna's Educational Views with Emphasis on the Education of Hygiene and Wellness. International Journal of Health Policy and Management, 1(3), pp.201–205.

lii Boyer, C.B. and Merzbach, U.C. (2011). A History of Mathematics. John Wiley & Sons.

liii Louis Charles Karpinski (1925). The History of Arithmetic.

liv Boyer, C.B. and Merzbach, U.C. (2011). A History of Mathematics. John Wiley & Sons.

lv Eisenstein, E.L. (2009). The printing press as an agent of change : communications and cultural transformations in early-modern Europe : vol. I and II. Cambridge: Cambridge Univ. Press.

lvi Anon, (n.d.). The Importance of Critical Thinking – Duke Learning and Organization Development. [online] Available at: https://sites.duke.edu/lodtraininghub/2020/11/19/the-importance-of-critical-thinking/.

lvii Wooldridge, A. (2021). ARISTOCRACY OF TALENT : how meritocracy made the modern world. S.L.: Allen Lane.

lviii Wooldridge, A. (2021). ARISTOCRACY OF TALENT : how meritocracy made the modern world. S.L.: Allen Lane.

lix Palace of Versailles. (2020). Versailles and the Royal Court. [online] Available at: https://en.chateauversailles.fr/discover/resources/versailles-and-royal-court#the-reign-of-louis-xiv.

[lx] Marco, P.P. (n.d.). The Travels of Marco Polo, Volume 2. Library of Alexandria.

[lxi] Edward B. Fiske, 'After 8 years of Open Admissions City College Still Debates Effects', NYT, 19th June 1978

[lxii] Wooldridge, A. (2021). ARISTOCRACY OF TALENT : how meritocracy made the modern world. S.L.: Allen Lane.

[lxiii] Wooldridge, A. (2021). ARISTOCRACY OF TALENT : how meritocracy made the modern world. S.L.: Allen Lane.

[lxiv] Wooldridge, A. (2021). ARISTOCRACY OF TALENT : how meritocracy made the modern world. S.L.: Allen Lane.

[lxv] Jessie Gregory Lutz (2008). Opening China : Karl F.A. Gützlaff and Sino-Western relations, 1827-1852. Grand Rapids, Mich.: William B. Eerdmans Pub. Co.

[lxvi] Wooldridge, A. (2021). ARISTOCRACY OF TALENT : how meritocracy made the modern world. S.L.: Allen Lane.

[lxvii] Willaim Deresiewicz, Excellent Sheep: The miseducation of the American Elite and the Way to a Meaningful Life (New York, Free Press, 2015), p. 210

[lxviii] Xiong, Q. and Ju, Y. (2022). Taoism and teaching without words. Educational Philosophy and Theory, pp.1–12.

[lxix] Marco, P.P. (n.d.). The Travels of Marco Polo, Volume 2. Library of Alexandria. (244)

[lxx] Ohkubo, K. and Kanariya Eiraku (2022). Talking About Rakugo 1: The Japanese Art of Storytelling. Kristine Stone Ohkubo.

[lxxi] Avildsen, J. G. (1984). The Karate Kid. Columbia Pictures.

[lxxii] Avildsen, J. G. (1984). The Karate Kid. Columbia Pictures.

[lxxiii] Avildsen, J. G. (1984). The Karate Kid. Columbia Pictures.

[lxxiv] Avildsen, John G. The Karate Kid. Columbia Pictures, 1984.

[lxxv] Peter Ducker, Harvard Business Review (1997), "The Future That Has Already Happened."

[lxxvi] Locke, E.A. (1982). The Ideas of Frederick W. Taylor: An Evaluation. The Academy of Management Review, 7(1), pp.14–24.

[lxxvii] Johnson, C. (2013). Painting the world pink. [online] Manchester Historian.

[lxxviii] (Masski Imai, 1986) Kaizen: the key to Japan's competitive success. Random House Business Division

[lxxix] European Union (n.d.). 1990-99. [online] european-union.europa.eu. Available at: https://european-union.europa.eu/principles-countries-history/history-eu/1990-99_en.

[lxxx] FCA. (2019). FCA fines Standard Chartered Bank £102.2 million for poor AML controls. [online] Available at: https://www.fca.org.uk/news/press-releases/fca-fines-standard-chartered-bank-102-2-million-poor-aml-controls.

[lxxxi] McKinsey & Company. (2020). From surviving to thriving: Reimagining the post-COVID-19 return. Retrieved from https://www.mckinsey.com/business-

functions/organization/our-insights/from-surviving-to-thriving-reimagining-the-post-covid-19-return

lxxxii Deloitte. (2020). COVID-19: Managing cash flow during a period of crisis. Retrieved from https://www2.deloitte.com/global/en/pages/about-deloitte/articles/covid-19/covid-19-managing-cash-flow-during-period-of-crisis.html

lxxxiii Rentschler, Eric. "The Fascination of a Fake: The Hitler Diaries." New German Critique, no. 90 (2003): 177–92. https://doi.org/10.2307/3211115.

lxxxiv Udemy, online education steps up: What the world is learning (from home) 2020.

lxxxv K.-L. Krause and H. Coates, "Students' engagement in first-year university," Assessment & Evaluation in Higher Education, vol. 33, no. 5, pp. 493–505, 2008.

lxxxvi Hoff, T. (2021). Covid-19 and The Study of Professionals and Professional Work. Journal of Management Studies, 58(5), pp.1395–1399.

lxxxvii University, S., Stanford and California 94305 (n.d.). The Architectural Treatise: Reading Like an Architect. [online] Leonardo's Library - Spotlight at Stanford. Available at: https://exhibits.stanford.edu/leonardo/feature/the-architectural-treatise-reading-like-an-architect.

lxxxviii C. Dunn, A. Wunnava (2019). The Effect of the Fukushima Nuclear Disaster on the Evolution of the Global Energy Mix. Harvard Kennedy School

lxxxix Anthony Klotz. Bloomberg (2021). "How to Quit Your Job in the Great Post-Pandemic Resignation Boom."

xc Parker, K. and Horowitz, J.M. (n.d.). Majority of workers who quit a job in 2021 cite low pay, no opportunities for advancement, feeling disrespected. [online] Pew Research Center. Available at: https://www.pewresearch.org/short-reads/2022/03/09/majority-of-workers-who-quit-a-job-in-2021-cite-low-pay-no-opportunities-for-advancement-feeling-disrespected/#:~:text=Overall%2C%20about%20one%2Din%2D [Accessed 8 Jun. 2023].

xcixci C. Newport (2021). Why Are So Many Knowledge Workers Quitting? [online] The New Yorker.

xcii De Smet, A., Dowling, B., Mugayar-Baldocchi, M. and Schaninger, B. (2022). Competition for talent after the Great Resignation | McKinsey. [online] www.mckinsey.com.

xciii De Smet, A., Dowling, B., Mugayar-Baldocchi, M. and Schaninger, B. (2022). Competition for talent after the Great Resignation | McKinsey. [online] www.mckinsey.com.

xciv Oliver, J. (2023). Half of big multinationals plan to cut office space in next three years. Financial Times. [online] 6 Jun. Available at: https://www.ft.com/content/276c26f2-889c-4e08-8f33-ce170890765b [Accessed 8 Jun. 2023].

xcv OpenAI (2023), Introducing ChatGPT, https://openai.com/blog/chatgpt

[xcvi] Future of Jobs Report (2023) World Economic Forum

[xcvii] OECD (2023), Is Education Losing the Race with Technology?: AI's Progress in Maths and Reading, Educational Research and Innovation, OECD Publishing, Paris, https://doi.org/10.1787/73105f99-en.

[xcviii] Future of Jobs Report (2023) World Economic Forum

[xcix] Johnson, B. (2017). English Coffeehouses. [online] Historic UK. Available at: https://www.historic-uk.com/CultureUK/English-Coffeehouses-Penny-Universities/.

[c] Gigerenzer, G. and Gaissmaier, W. (2011). Heuristic Decision Making. Annual Review of Psychology

[ci] Imperial College London. (n.d.). Unconscious bias. [online] Available at: https://www.imperial.ac.uk/equality/resources/unconscious-bias/#:~:text=Unconscious%20bias%20is%20triggered%20by.

[cii] Wargo, E. (2006). How Many Seconds to a First Impression? APS Observer, [online] 19(7). Available at: https://www.psychologicalscience.org/observer/how-many-seconds-to-a-first-impression.

[ciii] Kahneman, D. (2011). Thinking, Fast and Slow. New York: Farrar, Straus and Giroux. Pg 90

[civ] Blair IV. The Malleability of Automatic Stereotypes and Prejudice. Pers Soc Psychol Rev. 2002;6: 242–61.

[cv] Holt, J. (2011). Thinking, Fast and Slow — By Daniel Kahneman — Book Review. The New York Times

[cvi] Kahneman, D. (2011). Thinking, Fast and Slow. New York: Farrar, Straus and Giroux. Pg 417

[cvii] Ro, C. (2021). The complicated battle over unconscious-bias training. [online] www.bbc.com. Available at: https://www.bbc.com/worklife/article/20210326-the-complicated-battle-over-unconscious-bias-training.

[cviii] Kahneman, D. (2011). Thinking, Fast and Slow. New York: Farrar, Straus and Giroux.

[cix] Forrester Consulting. (2022). The Modern Workplace Demands a New Approach to Knowledge Management. Commissioned by Starmind.

[cx] Lipman, J. (2021). The Pandemic Revealed How Much We Hate Our Jobs. Now We Have a Chance to Reinvent Work. [online] Time. Available at: https://time.com/6051955/work-after-covid-19/.

[cxi] Inc, G. (2022). Is Quiet Quitting Real? [online] Gallup.com. Available at: https://www.gallup.com/workplace/398306/quiet-quitting-real.aspx#:~:text=%22Quiet%20quitters%22%20_____%20at.

[cxii] Hamel, G., & Breen, B. (2007). The Fut_____, MA: Harvard Business School Press.

[cxlii] Intentions (1891) 'The Critic as Ar_____

[cxiv] Percy, S. (n.d.). Do Extroverts Ma_____

[cxv] Wilmot, M.P., Wanberg, C.R., Kammeyer-Mueller, J.D. and Ones, D.S. (2019). Extraversion advantages at work: A quantitative review and synthesis of the meta-analytic evidence. Journal of Applied Psychology, 104(12), pp.1447–1470.

[cxvi] Matthew Syed, Viewpoint: Was CIA 'too white' to spot 9/11 clues?. (2019). BBC News.

[cxvii] www.linkedin.com. (n.d.). The Skills Companies Need Most in 2018 – And The Courses to Get Them.

[cxviii] Deloitte (2016). Global Human Capital Trends 2016 The new organization: Different by design. [online] Available at: https://www2.deloitte.com/content/dam/Deloitte/global/Documents/HumanCapital/gx-dup-global-human-capital-trends-2016.pdf.

[cxix] www.learningguild.com. (n.d.). Is Compliance Training Killing Your Learning Culture? : Learning Solutions | The Learning Guild

[cxx] Microsoft Industry Blogs - United Kingdom. (2019). How to introduce a learn-it-all culture in your business: 3 steps to success.

[cxxi] Amy C. Edmondson, The Fearless Organization: Creating Psychological Safety in the Workplace for Learning, Innovation, and Growth

[cxxii] Tom Westerling, Sysdoc. (n.d.). High Performing Teams - The Red Arrows

[cxxiii] Westfall, C. (n.d.). New Survey: Nearly Half Of Workers Unsatisfied With Learning And Development Programs. [online] Forbes. Available at: https://www.forbes.com/sites/chriswestfall/2019/10/08/new-survey-workers-unsatisfied-with-learning-and-development-programs-training-leadership/.

[cxxiv] Perspectives from independent learning practitioners IMPACT OF COVID-19 ON THE L&D PROFESSION. (2021).

[cxxv] Hurst, D.K. (1995). Crisis and Renewal.

[cxxvi] LinkedIn (2021). Workplace learning report 2020 | linkedin learning.

[cxxvii] Son, H.H. (2010) Human capital development, Asian Development Bank. Asian Development Bank. Available at: https://www.adb.org/publications/human-capital-development (Accessed: March 23, 2023).

[cxxviii] The importance of Digital Literacy for your workforce (no date) Go1. Available at: https://www.go1.com/blog/post-the-importance-of-digital-literacy-for-your-workforce (Accessed: March 23, 2023).

[cxxix] Bollard, A. et al. (2022) Accelerating the shift to a next-generation operating model, McKinsey & Company. McKinsey & Company. Available at: https://mckdev.mckinsey.com/business-functions/mckinsey-digital/our-insights/accele... ...ext-generation-operating-model ...essed: ...

...ources/2021-state-of-skills ...conomic Forum (no date). Available https://www3.weforum.org/docs/GCR2018/05FullReport/TheGlobalCompetitiv enessReport2018.pdf (Accessed: March 23, 2023).

cxxxii Bersin, Josh. "A New Paradigm For Corporate Training: Learning In The Flow of Work." Josh Bersin, June 2018.

cxxxiii Schacter, D.L., Daniel Todd Gilbert and Wegner, D.M. (2012). Psychology. New York: Worth Publishers.

cxxxiv Centrical. (n.d.). 'Learning in the Flow of Work' Is Just a Fad...If It Doesn't Work

cxxxv June 2023, A. feature 28 (n.d.). Unleashing the power of AI: transforming learning in the flow of work. [online] www.peoplemanagement.co.uk. Available at: https://www.peoplemanagement.co.uk/article/1827844/unleashing-power-ai-transforming-learning-flow-work [Accessed 31 Jul. 2023].

cxxxvi www.youtube.com. (n.d.). Charles Handy on Qualities of Vision and Leadership. [online] Available at: https://www.youtube.com/watch?v=KrR-OUSCWjE&t=1s

cxxxvii Pophal, L. (2021). The 100 Year History of the Human Resources Department | Visier Inc. [online] Visier, Inc. Available at: https://www.visier.com/blog/the-100-year-history-human-resources-department/.

cxxxviii Science Council (2019). Our definition of science. [online] The Science Council. Available at: https://sciencecouncil.org/about-science/our-definition-of-science/.

cxxxix Christer Thörnqvist, (2022), Human Resource Management: Scientific Theory Versus Pseudo- Scientific Practice in the Seminal Work by Belgian Sceptic Patrick Vermeren, n. Ann Soc Sci Manage Stud

cxl Christer Thörnqvist, (2022), Human Resource Management: Scientific Theory Versus Pseudo- Scientific Practice in the Seminal Work by Belgian Sceptic Patrick Vermeren, n. Ann Soc Sci Manage Stud

cxli Mel Green & Jake Young, Creating learning cultures: assessing the evidence, CIPD, April 2020

cxlii Argyris, C. (1977). Double Loop Learning in Organizations. [online] Harvard Business Review. Available at: https://hbr.org/1977/09/double-loop-learning-in-organizations.

cxliii Senge, P.M. (1990). The Fifth Discipline: the Art and Practice of the Learning Organization. New York: Doubleday.

cxliv Jac Fitz-Enz (2010). The new HR analytics : predicting the economic value of your company's human capital investments. New York Amacon 50's to the 62

cxlv piush.vaish (2016). Evolution of Strategic Management from 1950's to the modern day - A Data Analyst

cxlvi piush.vaish (2016). Evolution of Strategic Management from 1950's to the modern day - A Data Analyst cxlvii Reio, T.G., Rocco, T.S., Smith, D.H. and Chang, E. (2017), A Critique of Kirkpatrick's Evaluation Model. New Horizons in Adult Education and Human Resource Development, 29: 35-53.

cxlviii The Problem With L&D's Beloved Kirkpatrick Model (And What To Do About It). (2023). Forbes.

cxlix ALLIGER, G.M. and JANAK, E.A. (1989), KIRKPATRICK'S LEVELS OF TRAINING CRITERIA: THIRTY YEARS LATER. Personnel Psychology, 42: 331-342. https://doi.org/10.1111/j.1744-6570.1989.tb00661.x

cl GP Strategies, (2023) Measuring the Business Impact of Learning in 2023. Watershed

cli Whatfix (2022). Phillips ROI Model: The 5 Levels of Training Evaluation (2022) | Whatfix.

clii Bailey, A. The Kirkpatrick/Phillips Model for Evaluating Human Resource Development and Training

cliii Bailey, A. The Kirkpatrick/Phillips Model for Evaluating Human Resource Development and Training

cliv Biddlecombe, G. (2012) The Art of Rigging. [edition unavailable]. Dover Publications.

clv Biddlecombe, G. (2012) The Art of Rigging. [edition unavailable]. Dover Publications.

clvi Diaz, A. (2017). Trader slams Marc Faber: You have been so wrong, why are you right now? [online] CNBC. Available at: https://www.cnbc.com/2017/04/25/trader-slams-marc-faber-you-have-been-so-wrong-why-are-you-right-now.html

clvii Bates, A.W. (Tony) and Bates, A.W. (2015). 6.2 A short history of educational technology. opentextbc.ca. [online] Available at: https://opentextbc.ca/teachinginadigitalage/chapter/section-8-1-a-short-history-of-educational-technology/#:~:text=1%20Oral%20communication

clviii Eisenstein, Op. Cit., p. 432.

clix Clark, R.E. (2012). Learning from media : arguments, analysis, and evidence. Charlotte, Car. Du N.: Information Age Publishing.

clx Kozma, R.B., Shafika Isaacs and Unesco (2011). Transforming education : the power of ICT policies. Paris, France: United Nations Educational, Scientific And Cultural Organization.

clxi U.S. Department of Education, Office of Educational Technology, Artificial Intelligence and Future of Teaching and Learning: Insights and Recommendations, Washington, DC, 2023.

clxii Mitr

clxiii Cav19). The School in the Cloud. Corwin Press.

USA TO (n.d.). Microsoft CEO Nadella: 'Bots are the new apps'. [online] https:||ble at: bots-new com/story/tech/news/2016/03/30/microsof-ceo-nadella- 572/.

clxiv RSA (2010). RSA ANIMATE: Changing Education Paradigms. YouTube. Available at: https://www.youtube.com/watch?v=zDZFcDGpL4U&ab_channel=RSA

clxv Masie, E. (2006). Learning Rants, Raves, and Reflections: A Collection of Passionate and Professional Perspectives. Pfeiffer.

clxvi Donald Clark, *Personalised tutors - a dumb rich kid is more likely to graduate from college than a smart poor one* (June 2023) Donald Clark Plan B. [online] Available at: https://donaldclarkplanb.blogspot.com/search?updated-max=2023-06-23T13:39:00Z&max-results=13 [Accessed 21 Oct. 2023].

clxvii Amdur, E. (n.d.). 'The Illiterate Of The 21st Century...' [online] Forbes. Available at: https://www.forbes.com/sites/eliamdur/2022/10/04/the-illiterate-of-the-21st-century/.

clxviii Marquet, L.D. and Covey, S.R. (2013). Turn the ship around! : a true story of turning followers into leaders. London: Penguin Publishing Group.